BETTER
than
YESTERDAY

PROVERBS OF
A WOMAN'S
HEART

VICKI L. KEMP

Christian Living
B O O K S

Largo, Maryland

Christian Living Books, Inc.
P. O. Box 7584
Largo, MD 20792
christianlivingbooks.com
We bring your dreams to fruition.

ISBN Hardcover 9781562293550
ISBN Paperback 9781562293604

Printed in the United States of America

Library of Congress Cataloging-in-Publication Data on file

Cover and personal photographs by D Jordan Photographic

Endorsements

It is always a joy and a blessing to so many others when a woman is graced by God to be transparent and candidly express her innermost thoughts and emotions. Lady Kemp chronicles her journey and the transformational insight gained along the way!

—**Dr. Barbara McCoo Lewis**
International General Supervisor of Women,
Church of God in Christ

Self-help is a term that gained popularity over the last few decades. There's an entire section in major bookstores dedicated to self-help. But what you don't hear a lot about is self-care. And that is where this book shines. Lady Kemp, using her wealth of spiritual wisdom and personal experiences, has put together a work that is sure to help you take the necessary steps to rediscovering a life of complete wholeness. Take your time and read intently. This book will change your life.

—**Dr. Hart Ramsey, Sr.**
Senior Pastor and Founder, Northview Christian Church
Dothan/Montgomery, AL and Atlanta, GA

Better than Yesterday is a relevant and necessary devotional. The motivational messages from the Word of God provide daily tips and techniques to enhance the total person. This book will leave a lasting impact on your life while empowering your relationships in a positive way. These proverbs provide practical life lessons that if embraced will assist one in developing not only a better walk with God but also fulfilling one's kingdom assignment. This book will empower readers to reach their goals while empowering one for personal success.

—**Superintendent, Dr. Benjamin Stephens, III**
International Youth Department President, Church of God in Christ

Vicki Kemp is a beautiful woman with a heart that desires to be a blessing to many. Her passion for empowering women to become better than what they have experienced in their past is evident in her words and her walk. This book will bless and inspire you. Each proverb teaches a lesson on the importance of looking at life through the lens of God rather than our emotions and opinions. Take the Challenge at the end of each chapter and be honest with where you are in life. I believe that this book will aid in the pursuit of a better you!

—**Daniel Johnson**
Singer\Songwriter

For every woman who has said to herself, "I'm ready to move forward, to forgive, and heal," this book will give you the tools to do just that. Lady Vicki and I have been best friends, sisters, for over 35 years, and I am blown away by the content in this book. Having witnessed her journey up-close and personal, I still missed some of her struggles which were not revealed until reading this book. Her ability to challenge herself to be a true and better woman of God encourages and inspires me to take the necessary steps to press toward the purpose the Lord has on my life. I encourage you to take this book and apply truth to every area in your life that calls for change. Take the challenge and live *Better Than Yesterday.*

—**DeAnna Lewis, Franchise Owner**
Fatburger, Bakersfield, CA
French Fry Heaven, Phoenix, AZ
Milk n' Honey Gourmet Cereal, Los Angeles, CA
Wingstop Inc., Bakersfield, CA

As women, the most significant struggles we have in life are managing thoughts and resisting the dictates of our emotions. Thoughts of how others see us, thoughts that reflect on past hurts and disappointments and even thoughts that challenge the validity of our relationship with Christ are all tricks of the enemy to keep us distracted from the truth that in God's eyes we are wonderfully and fearfully made. The title of this book exposes thoughts that stem from traditionally held beliefs and from uncomfortable past experiences that have become not only the reference point for life challenges but also the regulator of our emotional state. As a Licensed Marriage Therapist, Minister, wife and mother, I encourage all women who are in need of mental and emotional healing to indulge in this anointed and timely book and begin to embrace the thoughts of a Proverbs 31 woman.

—Sheryl L. Brown, LMFT
Role Model Productions, Cumming, GA

What an honor it is to endorse my sister-friend, Lady Kemp's new book. I love the devotional style she uses to frame her chapters, giving each reader an opportunity to be introspective. I was moved by the context of forgiveness and freedom, as well as her call to respond differently to the obstacles that lurk from the past into our present and future. I pray that the audience of this book is provoked by the heartfelt proverbs which equipped her to attain many personal and spiritual victories. Lady Kemp uses the Word of God and the depth of her professional experience to guide the reader into harvesting the wisdom she intentionally leaves on a trail that forges forward throughout this proverbial compilation.

—Bridgett Barnes
Founder, Bridgett Barnes Ministries

According to Proverbs 12:13-14, the righteous come out of their trouble by their words. Regardless of the circumstances or crises you face in life, you can be victorious. This book will show you how to take God's promises and apply them to your life. Thank you, Lady Kemp, for letting God use you to minister hope to others and giving us the necessary tools to receive and maintain victory in our everyday lives.

—Martha L. Johnson
Pastor Emeritus
Compassion Christian Center
Bakersfield, CA

Dedication

This book is dedicated to those who have suffered the pain of rejection and feel their love wasn't good enough. To those who feel they can never overcome the very thing in life that was designed to destroy them. I applaud you; I cheer you on. By faith, you are better than yesterday.

My husband, Vernon Kemp, the love of my life, my greatest supporter, my king. I honor you. My life is better because you pushed me to become a stronger version of myself. I thank God for fashioning you just for me. All I desired to accomplish, you encouraged. Your godly wisdom helped me to complete this book of proverbs. I'm grateful for your love.

To my incredible children, I love you with all my heart. And to my angels, Alexandria Jourdin and Alexis Chrishone, you are my world, my gifts from God. Thank you for supporting and believing in me. I feel so favored that God blessed me to be your mother. You both are my teachers, gifted with brilliance. I'm excited to witness what you will do on the earth for God's glory. I love you dearly.

To my parents, Daniel Webster and Cora Jordan, who raised me to love God above all things. My loving father was a humble man of God who possessed strength and wisdom. He reminded me often that I was destined for greatness. My mom is a wonderful mother who makes sacrifices for so many. I am here, for she was here first. Your wisdom raised me to be loving and constant. I am that kingdom woman because of you. Proverb 22 is dedicated to you. I love you.

"I'm not getting older, I'm getting better."

Author Unknown

Contents

Foreword

The enemy is zealously on an assignment to destroy the people of God. He works relentlessly to keep us from moving forward in life and living. He attempts to create avenues for us to not only fail but wallow in failure. He crowds the lives of God's people with past issues and challenges in efforts to keep them stuck in their yesterday. Listen. We must not – we cannot – allow him to succeed. Now is a critical time to seek nonstop direction from God. The enemy steals our peace of mind by taking our focus off what is essential for our existence – deliverance. We must fight for our deliverance! Without a doubt, God is greater than the enemy. Period! The enemy tiptoes into our world with diminutive things, and he attempts to stop us by any means necessary in all areas of our lives. Be careful. Be watchful.

The enemy targets the mind and causes us to struggle against the power of principalities. We end up struggling with who we are as individuals and where we stand in our walk with God. The solution? Taking off the mask, looking in the mirror, and wholeheartedly facing the reality of who God created us to be. The solution rests in the newness of God and the new person we are in Him.

When dealing with past hurts, wounds, and strongholds, it's imperative to commit to strength. Commit to not being stuck. Choose to refuse to be emotionally trapped. Decree and declare that you will not live beneath your God-given privileges and become a new you! Jesus came that we might be prosperous, both naturally and spiritually. Jesus desires for us to be courageous and victorious in Him.

> Thou shalt also decree a thing, and it shall be established unto thee: and the light shall shine upon thy ways (Job 22:28).

Take control! You have been given authority to decree peace, wholeness, and sanctity in your life.

Better than Yesterday gives strategic insight into the enemy's strategies and real-world experiences that will force you to look inside yourself and expose those areas that long for a better you. You will be challenged to search your life and redefine those areas that have been masked and sealed for years. It's time to uncover those areas that are necessary for growth – areas of defeat, despair, unforgiveness, worry, pride, jealousy, negative thought patterns, pain, and regret. There is nothing too hard for our God! The power of the enemy is evident; however, we know this about our God: He is greater. 1 John 4:4 decrees, "For greater is He that is in me, than he that is in the world." God has all power.

I've learned that while in the midst of a relentless storm, it is important to give God the opportunity to speak to your soul. There is something He wants you to grasp and understand. Most of the time, God is trying to get us to understand that it's not about us – it has never been; it never will be. It's about bringing Him glory. How we go through is the predictor of how we come out. We bring glory to our Father when we weather the storm in faith, knowing He has a plan.

What do you do when you're waiting for the storm to be over? Trust in the Lord. When you can't figure out what God is doing, when His ways are incomprehensible, when what you see just doesn't seem to make sense, and His hand seems untraceable, just trust Him. Harness your emotions; speak to yourself; calm your spirit, and trust Him. Trust God. This incredible compilation of proverbs and testimonies will encourage you to do just that. It will teach you to look to God for all things.

I encourage you to welcome the challenges at the end of each chapter introspectively. In our journey to become better versions of ourselves, we must first identify areas of struggle to start the process of healing. We *can* be better than yesterday. Lady Kemp passionately reveals personal truths directly from her heart and exposes life stressors which have impacted her life that she might help others experience the beauty of peace, love, forgiveness, and newness. Her strategy of simplistic messaging and real-world examples gently invites you into her world. She does this while giving you the opportunity to see "the real," and actively apply truths to your life.

The important part of facing challenges is knowing that each circumstance you face is one that has the potential to develop you, mold you, enhance you, anoint you, and make you who you are to be in Christ – your destiny. Sometimes it might feel as if the tasks of the enemy were designed to take you out. When it appears you are going under, losing traction, and fighting for your breakthrough, God is in control. With Him, you can experience a better tomorrow. Good morning! Your new day is here! Enter in! Be faithful; keep moving forward and embrace the gift of God's restoration! You are better than yesterday!

–**Chrystal Rucker**
Gospel Recording Artist

Introduction

In my past, I was like a dandelion. I knew my place in the field. I was timid, easily hurt, and tossed apart by a gentle blow of the wind. God transformed me into a powerful rose; one that has finally found inner self-worth, strength, and acceptance. I am valuable to God.

Through the grace of God, I've grown in so many areas of my life. No longer am I easily broken. Now, I can endure the storms and rains of life because I've learned they're only present in my world, my pasture, for a season. I have bloomed in the midst of rejection and adversity, and have learned how to apply the principle of prayer. I've witnessed its power. I desire to encourage those who are struggling to overcome the strongholds of the enemy. I aspire to challenge them to apply the very principles that created the victory I now walk in. Through the miracle-working power of God, you can be the very best you. If placed in the right garden, you can also bloom.

God desires that we are whole and complete in every area of our lives. He does not want us to continue to hold on to past wounds as trophies and residue as bad memories. He wants us to be free – completely. He desires that we have champion states of mind and withstand the challenges of life on every level. It is possible through faith. Philippians 4:13 assures us that we can do all things through Christ who strengthens us. If you have the willingness to become better, you can. You simply need a made-up mind and relentless determination to WIN.

We have all experienced different walks of life; we all have different struggles that we continually fight to overcome. My struggle may have been different from yours, but it's a struggle. I've learned that the ultimate reward for defeating the struggle is the chance – the matchless opportunity to live without strongholds and in complete freedom. The goal is to remain free… totally free.

As you read the messages God gave me in this compilation, my prayer is that you look inward and release any and everything holding you back from *total* freedom. Speak words of life that stimulate inner healing and self-growth. Declare truths over every negative part of your life.

This book is a self-reflective guide birthed from my spiritual insights that were then constructed into a streamed consciousness format. It presents concepts that are thought-provoking and challenges self-defeating paradigms. I strongly encourage you to take on the challenge of self-evaluation and inner growth with confidence. Ignite that interpersonal dialogue to become a better you! As you visit each proverb, dissect and meditate on its insights. With God, you are far better than any past failures or hang-ups. All you need is courage to take a look within.

You don't have to be tied to the lies and tricks of the enemy. Our great God is a genius over every plan plotted against us. Satan has deceived us too long; we dare not continue to let him rob us of the freedom God promised in His Word! It is never too late to see yourself free through the eyes of faith.

Many are struggling, even in the church, although they are consistently hearing the Word. The struggle may seem unbearable because they have not challenged or applied truths to better their lives. This book will show you how to respond to the designs of the enemy – fiercely and confidently. Open your heart to God as you ask Him to change your perception of life and living. By faith, you are better – more than better – than yesterday.

Better than Yesterday Workbook

I encourage you to do the work.

The companion to *Better than Yesterday* will help you to gain a better understanding of the principles I share in this book and to fully incorporate them into your life. In a simple, yet, practical, interactive, self-reflective format, each Proverb contains…

♥ Thoughts to Ponder – Thinking from a Kingdom perspective

♥ The Challenge – Do you want to be better?

♥ Key Thoughts – Designing a strategy to defeat the enemy

♥ Kingdom Words – Words that empower you to be better

♥ Check Points – Checking yourself against the Word of God

This resource may be used by groups or individuals and can easily be adapted to suit the requirements for either. We long to forget the daunting memories of failure, poor choices, hurt, and regrets. As you progress through the workbook, ponder its truths and complete the exercises, you will develop the tools to defeat the enemy of your past and reach a better tomorrow.

ISBN 9781562293598   8.5" x 11"   54 pages   Paperback
Available wherever books are sold or from ChristianLivingBooks.com

PROVERB ONE

A CHALLENGE
—to FORGIVE and
LOVE

It was November. The air was crisp. Color was everywhere – red, green, and variations of oranges and yellows. As I drove through the mountains with my daughters, my eye drank in the canvas around me. God's masterpiece was stunning. I remember falling in love with God all over again. I stood in total awe of His creation. For a reason I cannot articulate, my spirit settled in the seat of forgiveness and love. I remember praying in the Spirit and asking the Lord to help me to genuinely forgive and love others as He commands us.

Life is precious. Fragile. Special. It is the living, breathing platform for God's work. Unlike the message that escapes our human, fallible rationale, life is always ripe to do the right thing, which is to forgive.

As the mountain hugged the skyline so beautifully that evening, my soul nestled in the bosom of my forgiving and loving Savior. It is because of His love for us – for me – that I have an example of true love.

The Message

Have you ever had the fretful experience of wallowing in regret? Was it an argument, an unpaid debt or a remark taken the wrong way? Maybe it was a message masked in miscommunication. Was your skin a little too thin that day? Do you remember at all? Do you remember that person? My friend, the weight of death is firm, and it is real. There is no round two. No second chances once death takes its place. No opportunity to make it right with that soul, to say, "I'm sorry" or "I love you." There is no rest in knowing you've been heard and understood. I imagine it's hard to remember. What began as a petty molehill somehow escalated into a mountain of who knows what, simply because neither of you chose to risk vulnerability for peace and love. No one sought forgiveness for the pure and simple sake of forgiving. You failed to reason. They chose to ignore your feelings. She blamed you. He never accepted his part in the problem. You both held on to strife. Whatever it was, it caused hurt and wreckage… enough to rip apart the very thing that was important to both of you. Somehow, now, life so short has ended so easily.

There are many things to keep in mind regarding forgiveness. We, God's children, must carefully identify the enemy's tactics and recognize when we allow him to do his work. When we become frustrated with ourselves and lash out at loved ones, our relationships can take a beating and end in strife. We must recognize when we give leeway to division and allow seeds of separation to take root. My friend, do not allow the enemy to steal your God-given relationships! Do not let him rent space in your heart where the love of God abides.

We must recognize when we give leeway to division and allow seeds of separation to take root.

The heart, the most vital organ in our human bodies, is at risk when we question forgiveness. The heart is essential to our existence. Naturally, we can't live without it. Spiritually, we need a heart transplant to live the abundant life God promised. The heart is the center of our beings, and its posture is a matter of utmost importance to God. Its condition must align with God's Word to successfully move forward in His will. Ignoring the spiritual condition of our hearts does not prevent our natural progression. In fact, we can still move forward, but we choose to do so without the full abundance of natural life God promises us on the earth.

You and I must grab hold of God's promises! We owe it to ourselves. Take the reins of your life and speak to your emotions. It is time to experience the gift of freedom our God provides to those who love Him and walk in His will!

My friend, it is important to recognize the need for forgiveness as it relates to our relationships. However, it is equally important to do so for the sake of freedom. Yes, freedom. True freedom. Forgiveness is freedom. When we seek to hold on to hurt, we rob ourselves of spiritually healthy lives.

My dear sister and neighbor, Janice Heard, was a strong champion of God. She went home to be with the Lord years ago. However, before she died, she ministered to me on many occasions. I remember her words so vividly, "Vicki, always forgive and allow nothing to stand before you and God. Unforgiveness can make you sick. Do not allow bitterness to take root in your heart. Forgive."

Life is vaporous. It's fragile and short. Why is it necessary to hold on to the weight of yesterday's hurts? Does it do you any good? Does it make you feel strong? Is there a lesson in it? If you think there is something to learn, take that lesson, leave the past behind, and forgive. Move on. Pray. Begin anew. The risks are too high, my friend. Life is too short. We cannot escape this reality; we must forgive.

> Then Peter came to Jesus and asked, "Lord, how many times shall I forgive my brother or sister who sins against me? Up to seven times? Jesus answered, "I tell you, not seven times, but seventy-seven times (Matthew 18:21-22).

FORGIVE.

Words of Life

Father, my heart is clean and love is flowing from and through it as You have created it to function. Thank You, Father, for a pure spiritual organ. I can live a long healthy life. Thank You, Father, that I walk in love and have a willingness to forgive as Your Word has instructed. Through Your Word, I am made free to live a greater life. I choose to trust You with my past, present, and future while learning to embrace all the greatness You have planned for me. I choose to forgive. I choose to love, and I am victorious. I am reminded of Your promise to me, "He healeth the broken heart, and bindeth up their wounds" (Psalm 147:3). I receive this promise in Your name.

The Challenge

Write down the names of the people, including yourself, whom you need to forgive and why. Pray. Breathe. Step outside of your comfort zone. Pick up the phone, write a letter or send an email. Do as your heart leads. Make peace with yourself and watch as the burdens of anger, frustration, resentment, fear, pride, and spiritual heaviness immediately lift. Open your heart to a world of freedom in Christ. David sought God personally and asked Him to, "Create in me a clean heart, O God; and renew a right spirit within me" (Psalm 51:10). It will be the same with your soul. You will have a right spirit. A new spirit. A whole new you.

PROVERB TWO
LET GO
to
LIVE

Women have heard the saying "let go to live" repeatedly, but the question is, how do I do that? What does that even mean, and where do I start? How does one let go when it feels much better to hold on to what we carry? Often, we refuse to let go because what we carry starts to feel normal. It's comfortable and natural. But it's a trap that keeps you from moving forward to live the very life God has planned for you.

The Message

Normal? How is that? You carried it so long it became part of who you are. You forgot bitterness, blame, and frustration are the fruits of unforgiveness because they were camouflaged by your comfort. I can relate. I have held on to hurt and constantly processed the very mistreatment I received from others. Regularly, I would press the rewind button in my mind, play the negative scenario all over again and hit pause. In those moments, I would meditate on the facts of the situation as *I* knew them. Often, I couldn't let go because I couldn't figure out the "whys." I would repeatedly ask myself, "What did I do *now*?" I would try to make sense of it all. I didn't realize I was feeding a victim mentality, wrapping and re-wrapping myself in an emotional security blanket.

Often, we think speaking our release is enough, but hurt and the remnants of mistreatment are rooted in our mental state. Being mentally and emotionally fragile forces us off balance and sinks us into a sea of self-pity. They cause us to hold onto past hurts and miss the blessed opportunity to live today. We hold on because somehow, we feel justified in holding on. Justified, yes! We continue to look back, rehearsing the hurt, replaying events over and over in our thoughts.

> *Being mentally and emotionally fragile forces us off balance and sinks us into a sea of self-pity.*

My reality was that I wanted to release it. I did. I knew it was not healthy for me. The problem was I didn't know how. I did not fully realize at the time I was falling into the enemy's trap. I bit the bait. I was dwelling on the message he wanted me to dwell on. He wanted me to get caught up in mind games, his prevalent scheme. The enemy takes pleasure in this strategy because it keeps us imprisoned by the hurt of yesterday. Nonetheless, I was reminded of the compelling story of Lot's wife. Deep within my spirit, I refused to be her. I refused!

> So it came to pass, when they had brought them outside, that he said, "Escape for your life! Do not look behind you nor stay anywhere in the plain. Escape to the mountains, lest you be destroyed." But his wife looked back behind him, and she became a pillar of salt (Genesis 19:17, 26 NKJV).

> Remember Lot's wife (Luke 17:32).

Lot's wife looked back. She disobeyed God's spoken command to keep her focus ahead. Looking back caused her to turn into a pillar of salt. This message in Luke was a warning to believers of Jesus Christ. Can you imagine what Lot's wife was thinking before she chose to look back? Maybe she was contemplating what she was leaving behind. Did she have regrets? What was pressing in her mind? Perhaps, she was second-guessing her decision to leave.

In your life, you will reach a point when you know it is time to let go. However, moving forward can be challenging when your past continuously calls you back. I'm sure before Lot's wife made her decision, she had questions about her past. The scripture does not tell us the details but just imagine. Imagine how many of us hold on because we feel we have the reasons and the right to do so. We hold on because our minds continually lock us into a painful cycle of rehashing the past. I've been there. I know what it's like to rehearse the hurts of yesterday and wallow in them. Furthermore, because the person on the opposite end did not own the wrongdoings, I continued to hold on because I felt I had every right to. Unfortunately, I continued to speak life into the wound and instead of it healing, it got worse. At times, I was close to recovery, but I would open the wound again as I shared my feelings with others and meditated on their opinions. Not only was this infecting the gaping hole that was once so close to healing, but I was sinking deeper and deeper into self-pity and hopelessness. That was a place I did not want to be in. It was such an unhealthy place.

As I grew older and wiser in my faith, I began to understand if I wanted to live, I had no choice but to let go. Ironically, what was so simple to understand, yet, challenging to accept was that people continued to live – really live – when I was stuck and stagnant in my walk with God. Letting go was a choice. We have a choice. You don't have to stay stuck! My healing was in my release. How did I do it? I began letting go of stuff, old, insignificant junk that was of no benefit to my life or my relationship with Christ. I stopped looking for people to own and validate my heartache and chose to own it myself. I acknowledged my pain and took responsibility for how I felt.

Dr. Hart Ramsey said it best, "Embrace the growing version of yourself. You have to grow thru to get to." I desired to be a better me and chose not to be a victim. I chose not to be a reflection of the pain I experienced. I refused to be a victim. I chose to grow. Mature. I chose to live.

Moving forward can be challenging when your past continuously calls you back.

Words of Life

Father, I release all weight to You, for there is no one greater than You. I release everything that is not of You. Your Word states in 1 John 4:4, "Ye are of God, little children, and have overcome them: because greater is He that is in you, than he that is in the world."

I am a champion in Christ Jesus, trusting the Father in every area of my life. I praise You, Father, for You will perfect all that concerns me. You will cause me to rise above my emotions, so I can continue to soar like the eagles. I cling to You, Father, more than ever, for You are the length of my days. I thank You, for today, I am a better me and tomorrow, I will be even better.

The Challenge

Write down any past hurts that continue to tug at your heart. How have they become emotional security blankets for you?

What do you need to release to grow? Be specific. Write it down.

PROVERB THREE
A KINGDOM WOMAN

Who am I? I am not what they say I am. I am a kingdom woman. A woman of the King Himself. I am a mirror of what I read in my Father's book. I am who God says I am, so why do I forget by acting contrary?

The Message

As women, why do we get caught up in the opinions of others? Why do we lose ourselves in how others feel about us? Non-factors. We get lost even further as we try very hard to prove we are not who they say we are. We lose ourselves in our attempts to show we are better than their assessments and definitions.

Listen. You are not who people say you are. You are better than their thoughts, accusations, and assumptions. Our parents, teachers, sisters, and clergy have exemplified the characteristics of marvelous women, who we are. We are a royal priesthood. We are the Queen Esthers and Marys, Lydias and Hannahs. We are the Ruths and the Deborahs. Unfortunately, we tend to forget this because we get lost in the sea of negativity. Don't drown in the belittlement and mystery of others. You must stand up and know who you are. You are what God has written on the pages of His Word. You are an overcomer. You are strong. You are an encourager who seeks to propel others to the next level.

As women, we ought to be intercessors seeking to pull our sisters and brothers up and out of the basement mentality that holds them captive to mediocrity. We are each other's strength. Do not get caught up in words that are irrelevant to your success. The apostle Paul says in Romans 3:4, "Let God be true and every man a liar." Lies. You can never trace them. I read a powerful quote:

> Your time is limited, so don't waste it living someone else's life. Do not be trapped by dogma – which is living with the results of other people's thinking. Do not let the noise of others' opinions drown out your own inner voice, and most importantly, do not lack the courage to follow your heart and intuition. – Steve Jobs[1]

That intuition, that gut feeling, that inner voice is Jesus speaking to us. We must listen and pay close attention to the details. Take heed. I recall times in my life when the words of others mattered to me. They were so important; they affected me emotionally. They confused my mind

---

1   http://thinkexist.com/quotation/your-time-is-limited-so-don-t-waste-it-living/406623.html

and tormented my spirit. I was so consumed by what other people said that I constantly questioned who I was in Christ. Therefore, I implore you not to let anyone devalue you. It is impossible to hear God if your focal point is on other people's assessments and opinions of you. The time has to come in your life when what they say or think doesn't matter. It's just noise and a subtle trick of the enemy to distract you. Stay focused but not on the noises. Declare who you are! A kingdom woman.

How can I begin to forget who I am when it is written in my heart and embedded in my mind? I had to remind myself that I am who God says I am. God defined my identity. I am all that I desire to be in Him. As I struggled with my identity and self-worth, I had to rehearse in my mind and speak to myself to reinforce this truth. I had to counter the negative thoughts by saying: "No, I'm not like that. That is not me. That is not who God says I am." At one point in my life, I felt the need to plead my case to naysayers in an effort to change their thoughts of me. I felt that pleading my case would help others see the character of Christ in me, rather than believing what others said about me.

As I began to grow in Christ and into a kingdom woman, those opinions no longer mattered. Their voices decreased until I heard none of the negativity. The conclusions they drew of me didn't matter. I meditated on the Word of God and conditioned my mind with *His* truths. The Word positioned me to a place of strength and confidence. It prepared me to stand strong in my thought life. Soon, the opinions of others compelled me to pray and seek the Lord, rather than seek to change what they thought of me.

Our minds can become so twisted trying to figure out the "whys" behind other people's thoughts. The enemy is sly and will relentlessly try to stop your progress. His main objective is to con you into believing a lie like he did with Eve in the garden of Eden. He wants to discredit God and the truth He speaks to you. In fact, Satan does not tell the truth. He is incapable of doing so:

> You belong to your father, the devil, and you want to carry
> out your father's desires. He was a murderer from the
> beginning, not holding to the truth, for there is no truth
> in him. When he lies, he speaks his native language, for
> he is a liar and the father of lies (John 8:44 NIV).

You are great! You need no one's opinion to validate who you are in the kingdom. I've discovered that the enemy intentionally seeks to assassinate everything that is honorable; nevertheless, when you have confidence in Christ, you have confidence in yourself. That's what matters.

Kingdom woman, I'm speaking to who you are in the spirit. I'm not referring to what people say about you but most importantly, where God wants to take you. There are many lessons to be learned before you can get to the next level. Therefore, it is essential to concentrate on pleasing Christ, the significant One. Who does God say we are? We are His children. This pronouncement is written on the pages of truth, His Word. Those righteous words reflect who we are. You need not prove anything to anyone but our great God. While others are trying their best to figure you out, spend your time developing a better you for the kingdom. Some people are not worthy of taking up the precious space in your heart and mind. Love yourself. Invest in you. Don't stop moving forward in the things of God because of others' false reflections of you. FALSE! They are non-factors, remember? Non-factors are barriers to your success – hindrances to who you are created to be in Christ. God will give you the ability to summit those mountains in your life that seem impossible. Keep pushing forward! Better is in your future. Your better is right now.

Non-factors are barriers to your success – hindrances to who you are created to be in Christ.

Words of Life

Father, I thank You that I hear Your voice; the voice of a stranger I will not follow. Therefore, I submit my will to You that I can operate effectively from the kingdom of God system. It's no longer I, but Christ who lives in me. His presence in my life will be evident in my home, on my job, in the community, and worldwide. I choose to live from the inside out, not from the outside in. I thank You for making and equipping me with tools of greatness to be an example of a kingdom woman. Today, I choose to focus on what You have said about me, not on the noise of others. I will not be distracted by the noise of the enemy because I have work to do in the kingdom. I decree and declare that I am a confident kingdom woman.

The Challenge

What past struggles have challenged your confidence? Explain.

What hindrances are you currently facing which stop you from moving forward and becoming a better you? Evaluate why.

PROVERB FOUR
UNLIMITED
POSSIBILITIES

Do you sit and ponder the possibilities in your life? Do you meditate and waste time dreaming about what you *may* be able to do in the future. God has told you to do great exploits in the earth realm. He has given you unlimited possibilities. You have the God-given ability to go further and well beyond your expectations. With God, all things are possible.

The Message

Think about it. We waste time resisting what God has instructed us to do. If we never start, we are guaranteed never to finish. The enemy fights us hard with distractions that cause us to lose focus. He is good at what he does; he is a mastermind at deception. He is exact in his pursuits and diligent when working towards killing your passion. Your passion is the motivator and zest that pushes you to win, reach, grow, and give. Passion is your energizer. It keeps you grounded and moving forward. The enemy will create situations and cause you to lose heart by discouraging you from the task that is in motion. We must not allow the enemy to go unchecked. Check him! He must be stopped. He is confident; therefore, we must be even more confident. According to Matthew 14, while Peter was walking on water, stepping out on faith, he was secure. When he took his eyes off Jesus, he became unfocused and mesmerized with fear; it was then he began to sink.

> *We must not allow the enemy to go unchecked. He is confident; therefore, we must be even more confident.*

That's a great lesson: keep looking forward, keep moving, and remain focused. Be cognizant of the fact that fear is not your ally. Rather, it is a ruthless enemy. Fear has no face. Therefore, the feeling of fear is threatening. Remember that. Jesus instructed Peter to walk on the water. Peter started out fearlessly. Period. However, even though the Creator of the universe instructed him to walk on the sea, the "what ifs" in Peter's life caused him to question the validity of God's words. As he began to think and question God's ability, he started to sink. God had already paved the way for his success. He could not fail as long as his focus stayed on the Almighty. Regardless of what you see, keep the faith. Faith believes in what appears impossible.

What's around you is not important. Water. People. Mountains. Whatever. You have work to do. What are you afraid of? What holds you back? Have no fear and continue to walk on the Word, for God has also lifted you above failing. By chance, if you should fail, get back up and try again, having learned invaluable lessons. We often look at failing as a bad thing; however, it is a stimulus to get it right the next time. No one can do for you what God has done, so don't allow the enemy to win. Beat him at his game. With the Word of God's authority, you have what is needed to check him and put him in his place. He belongs under your feet, not above you.

We are greater than the enemy's plots, tricks, and plans. We are greater than the enemy's plots, tricks, and plans. No, it's not a typo. Sometimes, we must hear something continuously until we believe it. Continue to tell yourself that the enemy will not keep you in a holding pattern. Speak life to yourself. Break the pattern of starting and not finishing. Break the pattern of being lazy and complacent. Break the pattern of being satisfied and always settling for less than. Stop making excuses. Break the pattern of being inconsistent and disobedient. You can't get things done by just talking. You must take a step in faith and finish. Be a finisher. A closer. Don't leave projects undone. The very thing you have not completed is the very thing that will save someone's life. Remember, we are victorious, and we triumph in Him. In Him, the Author of Completion, there is no failure.

God has given us many gifts to be blessings to others; however, we often sit and become stagnant, not using the gifts God has given us. He has graced us with wisdom, tools, innovative ideas, and the ability to perform and be great. We must stop dreaming of implementing our dreams and start putting dreams into action. Start now. Today.

We must stop dreaming of implementing our dreams and start putting dreams into action.

Your dream may feel like a massive undertaking; nevertheless, you have ambition, stamina, and wit. You have everything needed to be at the top! God has also graced you with creative ability, for His Word has creative power.

> So shall my word be that goeth forth out of my mouth: it shall not return unto me void, but it shall accomplish that which I please, and it shall prosper in the thing whereto I sent it (Isaiah 55:11).

Courageous faith. The very thing you're trying to create has already been done by faith. Faith is trust, confidence, and conviction. The possibilities are unlimited. Unrestricted. Speak to it, and watch it come to pass. Your beginning, your blessing, and your ending are in your mouth, so speak it. Faith backs your words. Victory is your commonplace. Yes, I said victory, so count it done! According to the Word of God, you will victoriously produce a greater harvest. The Word is the final authority in all matters. You have the strength and the wherewithal to produce. The breath of God is behind you pushing you forward, onward, and upward! Defeat is not in your pedigree. Doubt and unbelief are taken out of your vocabulary. Watch your thoughts and your words! It is so imperative to speak words of life. Our thoughts must line up with God's Word for victorious results. One of my faith mentors, Lilli Parker, often tells me, "For me to fail, impossible! You have what you say." What are you saying? What are you believing? What are you speaking into the atmosphere? Is it good? Is it right? Is it for you? Is it dripping with faith?

You have a renewed mindset by faith. Faith does not only believe; it also knows. Faith even exists in the absence of proof. The lack of faith is an assassinator of your dreams and visions. Verbal faith is not enough; you have to see it although it has not produced or manifested yet. Faith endures and obeys the Word of God. You got this! Be confident in the incredible God you serve. He moves mountains, and He performs miracles.

I'm sure you've heard the old saying, "God is your copilot," but our great God is more than a copilot; He is your pilot. He is with you driving the plane of your life, helping you with each task, dream, and vision. He is composing, rearranging, maneuvering, and shifting everything negative you can't see. God is your enthusiast. Move forward with your kingdom agenda. Make your brand, and don't waste time dreaming of the fear of the unknown. Stop questioning how the provision will be made. How will I approach this task? How do I birth the dream that was given to me? Yes, it's okay to have questions. You're human, so naturally, you will want to question the what-ifs. However, when your mind gets flooded with endless questions, your faith becomes drowned in noise. Silence your mind and startle your faith. Remember the One who controls the ins and outs of your everyday life. Let me encourage you. God will download the information you need and coach your every move. You will have everything you need to triumph. And listen, don't be apprehensive about people not validating you. It's OK; you just keep pushing. Keep your eyes focused on what you need to get accomplished.

I heard a powerful speech by actress Aja Naomi King. She stated, "In order to thrive, we have to stop believing that the root of our talent is a tree growing in someone else's yard as if the fruit it bears don't belong to me."[1]

---

1   https://www.essence.com/video/aja-naomi-king-essence-black-women-hollywood-speech-self-doubt

You have to tell the enemy, "It belongs to me, and you can't have it!" Your God-given ability belongs to you! The dream God gave you belongs to you, so you make it come alive. You plant it; you water it. Don't lose sight of what God gave you, and don't give your dream to someone else. You can do this! Don't just continue to dream. Execute. Accomplish. Move. Dreaming is powerful; however, you can become complacent and comfortable. There's safety in that boat. Execution is risky. Think about it. The possibility of failing is painful and disappointing. If others knew we failed, it would be humiliating, so we stay stuck, stagnant, unproductive, shackled in fear and disconnected from the life God wants for us. God desires that you WIN. You are victorious! Stay on the course. God counterbalances all of your losses.

With God's favor, there are unlimited possibilities. What God has placed in each of us is valuable – a true threat to the enemy's domain. The enemy is overpowered, and what God has given you will cause his domain to fail and not prosper. You are powerful, yes you are. His plan in your life won't work. The good news is we are pregnant with unlimited possibilities just waiting to be birthed. Believe in yourself even when the odds appear to be against you. All that you aspire to be, you deserve, so push through that mentality of doubt. Be brave; you got this. There is no need to worry about the provision, for it is made. You will be successful. Step by step, execute by faith. The enemy's plan for us to fail is canceled in the name of Jesus. Be encouraged by Luke 1:37, which says with God all things are possible. Therefore, every negative expectation planted by the enemy is abolished. I encourage you to open your spiritual eyes and see all the unlimited possibilities God has given you. Move forward quickly, boldly, and triumphantly. In faith, know that He is working behind the scenes on your behalf.

You can do this! Don't just continue to dream. Execute. Accomplish. Move.

Words of Life

Father, I thank You for giving me the mentality to win and not fail; therefore, I will execute by faith what You have assigned me to do. I decree and declare that I am strong-minded. As Your Word reads in Philippians 4:13, "I can do all things through Christ which strengthened me." I decree that I am a winner. I will not be distracted but will succeed as Your Word has promised because Your Word works! I thank You that I already see what You have placed in my spirit to complete. I am grateful that You are already at work in every area of my life. I already see the promises of God manifested.

The Challenge

What has distracted you from achieving your God-given dreams?

Find a scripture that encourages you to release the God-given passion that will encourage you to succeed in life. Write down your confession. Revisit it daily.

PROVERB FIVE
LOVE YOU – STILL

L ove is an emotion that surpasses a multitude of faults and cancels out fear. It is the emotion that conceals matters when situations lead to bitterness. It is the feeling that causes one to act when the flesh and mind say, "Stop. No. I'm done."

The Message

Love is the greatest teacher. Opening your heart to love others is one of the greatest attributes given to human beings by God. Giving of yourself and forgetting all biases and prejudices demonstrates true love at its core. Love protects and shields. And, when we choose to see through the eyes of our Father, we are given the gift to love beyond faults. It is truly a beautiful thing. Have you ever witnessed the miraculous power of love? Have you loved someone in spite of their shortcomings? Can you see the person's attributes, pettiness, faults, mistakes, and mishaps, and choose to love them – still? Maybe it's easier to see through the opposite lens by considering yourself. Take a moment to think about *your* faults, imperfections, and flaws. Nevertheless, despite these issues, struggles, and even drama, someone chooses to love *you* – still. Love doesn't get much better than that.

Love is me choosing to see you and you choosing to see me. It is recognizing that you are not perfect; that we all have faults. We have all hurt others at one point or another, but when someone hurts us, we deem it a misdemeanor, maybe even a felony depending on the level of pain we feel. Oh, how quickly we forget that no one is perfect. Sometimes, we settle in a protective space and comfort ourselves by saying, "I'm done. They will never hurt me again. They will never have the opportunity to trample on my heart again." We sometimes forget God, Himself, loves us with unconditional love; so much so that He gave His life that we might live. We are living because of God's amazing love! That alone is a beautiful thing!

Love is a word regularly said and preached about in the church but not often shown. We speak the words "I love you," but at times, we fail to demonstrate the love we speak so confidently about. Actions scream what you are unable to say, audibly. Give a warm hug. Let your neighbor feel it. Smile. Share your time. Have a conversation and occasionally, if the time is right, give your finances. Love. And love like you mean it. Love is mature; love is real, and love is honest.

Actions scream what you are unable to say, audibly.

Love me; don't mistreat me. Love me; don't judge me secretly. Respect and handle me as God handles me… gently and kindly. Galatians 5 teaches about the fruit of the Spirit, which are explanations of God's nature. As His children, such qualities should be exhibited in our lives. Love me and push me to my destiny by encouraging me to be better. Love from a genuine place with pure (untainted) motives. This agape love I speak about can only be gained through a relationship with God. Having a relationship with God empowers you to love unconditionally, not because the preacher tells you to. Through faith in Jesus Christ, we love, even when it is uncomfortable. Uncomfortable! Yes, you love your sister and brother even if they have issues with you. You love them – still. Although you tried to make amends, they were not ready to receive your love, but you owe love – still. Although they have been cruel, you owe love – still. Listen, I didn't say hang out with them, and I didn't say run behind them. I didn't say remain connected to them. I didn't say be a doormat for them. I said you simply owe love – still. Yes, because the Word of God says so. Period.

The world watches us as believers. Let me remind you of this scripture:

> By this shall all men know that ye are my disciples if
> ye have love one to another (John 13:35).

Ask yourself a question, "What does your love look like?" Love sees beyond what the enemy tries to root in the heart. Love is bigger than the issues. The love of God uproots all negativity by looking through the eyes of Jesus and seeing your sister and brother as Jesus sees them. Blemished. Not perfect. They are human. By the power of the Holy Ghost and living by the principles of the Word, we conquer. Through the Spirit of Christ, we can love like we are designed. We can love and look for nothing in return. And when motives are in true alignment with the Word of God, when there are no accolades needed and no hidden agendas – true love takes root.

> Charity suffereth long and is kind; charity envieth not; charity vaunteth not itself, it is not puffed up (1 Corinthians 13:4).

God is love, so I must show love. God's love is shown throughout the scriptures countless times. Love causes us to remember when we didn't have it together ourselves. As a result, it is easier to be patient and long-suffering. Don't forget – you were not always saved and mature. Reflecting on the book of Matthew 26, Judas betrayed Jesus for thirty pieces of silver, and Jesus loved Judas – still. Also in Matthew 26, Peter denied Jesus three times, but Jesus loved him – still. Honestly, it can be difficult to love once you are hurt. Very difficult. Tough. Problematic. Awkward. But through Christ, you can love – still. You may find it difficult to love in your strength; however, you can love in the strength of the Lord.

In the event you are ever mistreated, you owe love – still. If you are ever used up and talked about, you owe love – still. The people you have helped the most, if they choose to forget, betray, and count you worthless, you owe them love – still. Although heartbroken, you owe love – still.

> Owe no man anything, but to love one another: for he that loveth another hath fulfilled the law (Romans 13:8).

Will you fulfill the law? This is a personal question that only you can answer. The Word of God gives you the capacity to love beyond how others have treated you, for God's love is not based on condition. Do you base your love on conditions, circumstances, status or emotions? Think about it. The love of God will stretch you to be more accepting of those who have not yet matured in Christ. Love is powerful, reaching into the heavens and touching the very heart of God. Love teaches us to feed our enemies and pray for those who deceived you. Yes, deceived you. Sacrificial love is a demonstration of who God truly is. Behind this four-letter word is a great sacrifice. It encompasses a strong emotion, which represents unselfishness. It requires you to give more of yourself solely for the welfare of another. And when giving of yourself, your heart is genuine; it is pure. It is love that keeps us secure and devoted to one another, even in the midst of a fiery trial. It is love that causes us to understand another's point of view even when the true content of the heart is revealed.

> *It is love that keeps us secure and devoted to one another, even in the midst of a fiery trial.*

> For God loved the world so much that he gave his one
> and only Son, so that everyone who believes in him
> will not perish but have eternal life. (John 3:16 NLT).

This scripture is our demonstration of love to the greatest degree. Think about all the times God has rescued us from a horrible place of sin. His mercy and grace were rich towards us. Think about the times you *knew* you did not deserve a second chance, but our great God gave you favor to live and not die. He gives us so many chances to get it right because of the love He has for us.

> But God demonstrates his own love for us in this:
> While we were still sinners, Christ died for us
> (Romans 5:8 NIV).

That's true love. Agape love. That's love that flows freely despite who we are or what we do. It is the type of love that gives – still.

Words of Life

Father, I walk in love from my heart, and I mean it. Father, I thank You that it is difficult for me to get offended, and it is easy for me to forgive. I not only speak love from my lips but love is displayed in my deeds. I demonstrate love as Your Word commands me to. Father, I thank You for giving me the strength to love those who have hurt and mistreated me. I am better because of Your Word. It is Your love that keeps me sane. It is because of Your love that I also see myself. It is because of Your agape love that life is sweet. For those who have done me wrong, I speak nothing but blessings over them. In Jesus' name. Amen.

The Challenge

What has hindered you from loving others as the Word commands?

Describe how you feel and what step(s) you must take, according to the Word, to walk in victory.

Read 1 Corinthians 13:1-13. What attribute of love is missing in your life? Contemplate why.

REJECTION

Rejection causes a numbing sensation that forces us to withdraw and shut down. From where do I draw strength when I continuously feel abandoned and skipped over by my peers? How do I overcome feelings of inferiority and not being good enough? God is my help. He strengthens me to face those who have rejected me. I am healed, for He is my healer.

The Message

Rejection is an incredibly strong emotion. The feeling of not being accepted can affect your happy place, leaving you feeling withdrawn, closed, and isolated. Your self-esteem is affected and you question your self-worth. This causes you to wonder why you are not accepted: "Am I not good enough to fit into the social clique? Maybe the folks just didn't like me."

Thoughts like these can leave you feeling as if you just don't measure up. Sometimes it gets worse. Truth is you may feel rejected by someone you thought loved you, only to find out later you did not need that person like you *thought* you did. You realized you need no one to affirm you. The validation you thought necessary was rejected – in a good way. Little did you know the rejection was designed to bless and make you better. Ponder for a moment. How did you allow the situation to affect you?

Sometimes, our thoughts can get in the way. We spend too much time dwelling on the pain birthed from the experience. Eventually, we start evaluating and measuring ourselves against the ones who rejected us. That is incredibly unhealthy. No one is immune to rejection, but we all have a choice as to how we handle it. That's the vital part. Will you allow rejection to stop your progress? Will you rehearse the initial feeling over and over again? Will you let the rejection determine your attitude, good or bad, and dictate how you respond to others (innocent ones) in your presence?

> *Eventually, we start evaluating and measuring ourselves against the ones who rejected us.*

In Mark Chapter 14, Jesus was the guest of honor at a get-together. As Jesus was eating, Mary entered the room with a special alabaster box of perfume. It was a regular practice to wash the feet of a guest. However, Mary went beyond the custom, broke the container of special perfume, and poured it on Jesus' head. Immediately, the disciples criticized her. They were upset and filled with resentment. Interestingly, they had the nerve to be angry because they believed she wasted the perfume. They felt she could have sold it or given it to the poor. It's amazing how others are so bold to have opinions about what they think *you* should do, right? Don't let the opinions of others minimize or negate what you have been assigned to do. Opinions, when compared to the Word of God, are dangerous. A person's opinion is not a law. If they knew your story, they would not throw shade on your glory.

I've also discovered that people who criticize you will try to make you feel smaller than they are, so they feel better about themselves. They will try to keep you hidden on the back side of the mountain because of their own intimidation. Don't you see? It's their problem, not yours. Rejection is sometimes God's way of protecting us. Think about it. (Sigh)

When you know who you are and Whose you are, it doesn't matter what people think. Mary was rejected too. A good thing, a kingdom thing, was rejected. Have you ever tried, hard, to love somebody, and they spurned your love? They rejected your hugs and your smile. Have you ever apologized but found it wasn't good enough? They turned their backs on you. They wouldn't give you a moment of their time. They made you feel like you weren't important enough for their attention. You were made to feel you weren't smart enough, not pretty enough. You didn't dress the part. You didn't drive the right car, or you weren't articulate enough. Rejected, yes, but accepted by God nevertheless. You are royal – queenly. Sometimes, you have to remind others who you are and why you will accept nothing less than what God expects you to receive.

You are reminded of who you are in the following scripture:

> But you are a chosen people, a royal priesthood, a holy nation, God's special possession, that you may declare the praises of him who called you out of darkness into his wonderful light (1 Peter 2:9 NIV).

You are a royal priesthood, so others should be careful how they handle you. You may not get 1,000 likes on Facebook or Instagram, but one like from God is sufficient. It is enough.

Today, if you are struggling with rejection, despite the pain, you must give God your all. Give it to Him today. My own experiences have taught me the importance of not letting rejection hold me hostage to the feelings and expectations placed upon me. Don't be concerned about those who reject you or don't accept your gift. Why? It's a roadblock designed to be an emotional hindrance. It's intended to discourage you, to get into your spirit and keep you from moving forward in the things of God. One thing I love about those who reject me is that they take me to a place in God where my friends can't take me. They cause me to get on my knees and seek God even the more.

Stop trying to make it all make sense. It won't. Some things just don't make sense. If you let it, rejection will keep you running in circles. It will keep you up at night stressing, thinking… processing. What I love about Mary is that she was focused. Unbothered. Anointed. It takes the anointing to carry you when you are in the midst of rejection and unacceptance. She had to be focused because she was in a room filled with negativity, murmurings, and complaints; however, she pressed past it. Think about it. You know what it's like to walk into a room with your heart in a good place. You begin to look around and hear side conversations and whispers. When you are dealing with people who find fault, prideful people, strong personalities, and demon-infested people who look for problems to criticize, you must wear spiritual armor to stay protected at all times.

Stand firm then, with the belt of truth buckled around your waist, with the breastplate of righteousness in place, and with your feet fitted with the readiness that comes from the gospel of peace. In addition to all this, take up the shield of faith, with which you can extinguish all the flaming arrows of the evil one. Take the helmet of salvation and the sword of the Spirit, which is the word of God (Ephesians 6:14 -17 NIV).

At some point in your life, you will come face-to-face with rejection. The day that happens, you have a choice. Instead of taking revenge with words and physical weaponry, use the weapons that come directly from God. You must have power – the power to stand strong and to keep moving forward. In spite of what you're up against (because it doesn't matter what you're up against), God plus one is the majority. If He is for you, who shall be against you?

Mary moved forward; she focused on getting to Jesus. She conquered what came against her – rejection. And so must you – rejected but accepted by God. You are royalty. Let nothing hinder you – no demon, no giant, no person, not one spirit of rejection. Let nothing separate you from the love of God. Nothing.

Rejected, yes, but accepted by God nevertheless. You are royal – queenly. Sometimes, you have to remind others who you are and why you will accept nothing less than what God expects you to receive.

Words of Life

Father, I thank You for Your healing. I am healed from the spirit of rejection. I will no longer be held back by those who do not accept me. I will remind myself daily that I am royalty, and I sit in heavenly places. I will walk with my head held high for I am free. Thank You, Lord, for accepting the godly gifts I present to You. I will remain focused on You and not on the critiques of others. I praise You for my new-found freedom.

The Challenge

How has rejection made you feel?

How can you overcome past rejections according to the Word? Explain.

How long have you allowed yourself to walk in rejection?

What may have prevented you from seeking help or insight from a trusted friend, family member or counselor?

NEGATIVITY BREEDS *an* UNTAMED MINDSET

A mind mingled with unkind, bitter thoughts is shaped by its focus on insignificant things. Time, when lost, cannot be recouped. With God's Word, you can get back to a positive place.

The Message

One tactic of the enemy is to use our thoughts against us. How do you stay positive in a negative world? Change the channel in your mindset. Don't rehearse the negative. It's a trick to keep you trapped. When the enemy presents a wicked thought, cast it down immediately because a thought is only a thought until you bring it to life. If you bring the thought to life, and it becomes a living organism. You are creating, not just a movie scene, but the soundtrack and the graphics. Don't let the enemy sit upon the seat of your emotions, infiltrate your thought life, and render you incapacitated. The Word of God gives us the strategy to stay mentally tough against him.

> Finally, brethren, whatsoever things are true, whatsoever things are honest, whatsoever things are just, whatsoever things are pure, whatsoever things are lovely, whatsoever things are of good report; if there be any virtue, and if there be any praise, think on these things. Those things, which ye have both learned, and received, and heard, and seen in me, do: and the God of peace shall be with you (Philippians 4:8-9).

The enemy's desire is for us to war with his lies; thus, creating unnecessary confusion in our minds. Nevertheless, we are empowered by God's Word to destroy vain imaginations. That negative thought can't go higher than God's Word. Guard yourself! Don't play on the enemy's turf. The devil doesn't play fair. He's evil and will attempt to destroy us by any means necessary. The mindset of a child of God is focused on things above. How do you remain positive when there is violence, warfare, death, depression, foreclosure, divorce, depleting health, and poverty all around you? Rest in God – outside of your situation! The only tool the devil has to use against us is our situation. He's not all-powerful; therefore, he's not worthy of the power he commands. He wants to constantly remind you that you are defeated because of your circumstances.

We live in a time in which we are incessantly reminded of the world's problems. Moreover, we are consumed with trying to figure out what

God has already worked out. It's already done. The enemy's suggestions are insignificant. They are intended to cause confusion, so it is not necessary to entertain them. The devil creates smoke screens to confuse and keep us in bondage. His trick is to torment our minds. He creates illusions for the pleasure of people, untruths rooted in deception. Hence, the Word of God cautions us to be watchful.

> Keep thy heart with all diligence; for out of it are the issues of life (Proverbs 4:23).

The heart encompasses the mind and all that comes from it. Protect your heart and govern it with the Word of God. Most importantly, when a thought enters the forefront of your mind, remember to examine it by the standard of the Word of God. Depending on how it measures up, you can accept the thought or choose to reject it. We are given the freedom and power to choose. It is important that we do so wisely.

I recall a time in my life when I was ill for a year-and-a-half diagnosed with functional dyspepsia. I was hospitalized on several occasions and had to undergo tests before this diagnosis. I could not eat, which caused me to lose a significant amount of weight and I was constantly in pain. I had adverse reactions to the medications prescribed by the gastroenterologist, which worsened my condition. After being told by the gastroenterologist that there was nothing further he could do to help me, he suggested I get a second opinion.

The enemy gets a kick out of knowing you're sick. He is tickled even further when even specialists cannot find the source of the symptoms. I was so fearful. I feared the unknown. I remember calling a dear friend, Marisa Banks. As soon as she answered the phone, I said, "Friend, I'm scared." There was no questioning me; she instantly started praying and pleading the blood over my mind. She commanded, with authority, that the torment of fear and the buffets of Satan be stopped immediately. Satan was laughing at me. He laughs, but remember, he won't laugh for long.

I will never forget the day I was in my doctor's office for a scheduled visit and was told I had symptoms of stomach cancer. Audibly, I said to her: "I don't receive that." I said it loudly!

The enemy attempts to reach way back in the past and dig up areas that are covered in the blood of Jesus; however; it's null and void! I was mentally tormented by what she said because my mother had stomach cancer when she was in her forties, and at the time, I was in my forties. My thoughts began to rage even louder and louder, but I remembered my mother often declaring that the fruit of her body would always be blessed. I am her fruit, a recipient of her grace and healing. She was completely healed of stomach cancer over forty years ago. Although shaken, I was standing on those words.

I underwent two procedures to confirm or negate the diagnosis. During the two weeks, while waiting for the results, the enemy worked hard to torment me with discouragement, doubt, and "what if" thoughts. At times, I entertained those thoughts. Other times, I threw them back into the pit of hell. I received the call from the doctor's office, and I was asked to come in for a review of the results. Almost immediately after receiving the call, the enemy's voice got louder in my mind. I caved into negative thoughts in a matter of seconds.

I called my husband, "Dear, my results are in. Can you come with me to the appointment?"

He responded, "Go in faith; you will be fine. Trust God for the outcome."

Shaking, I snapped back at him, "You're kidding – you're not going with me?"

That was not going to work! I wanted – needed – someone to be with me. The thoughts continued to race. Looking back on the experience, I now see the enemy's plan. He wanted to cloud my mind with fear. Fear will paralyze you if you let it. My mother met me at my doctor's office. I got the results. I did not have cancer! I was overcome with relief.

As I headed to my car, I saw my husband in the parking lot. All along, I didn't know he had followed me there. I nearly yelled as I shared the test results with him across the parking lot. He responded with hugs and a smile, "God is faithful. You have to rely on your faith and not the lies of the enemy." Your faith, not your mother's faith, not your husband's faith but your faith.

There may be times when you need to ask God to help your faith factor. It may appear that the facts are prevailing, but faith must be your stance. You must simply change the channel in your mind to a picture of peace and faith in our Lord Jesus. God is faithful. He is sovereign over all the powers of the enemy.

What a reminder! I already knew the devil was a bully, but I needed the reminder. I almost allowed him to dominate! The enemy loves to take our thoughts to the point of no return and cause us to be caught up in negative thought patterns. You must speak out loud, with authority, and tell the enemy that he will not have power over your mind. He is defeated!

You must tell the enemy that he will not have power over your mind. He is defeated!

> God has not given us a spirit of fear, but of power and
> of love and of a sound mind (2 Timothy 1:7 NJKV).

A sound mind, indeed. The mind is a battleground, and our victory is the Word of God. It's our matchless weapon. Having a strong mind takes work. It takes considerable effort. It takes consistency. Commit to be free. Don't you think you are worth it? Decide to be whole. Dig into the Word of God for freedom. Don't stay stuck in demonic thought patterns, demonic deceptions, unreal truths, unrealistic games, and lies. To get free and stay free, we must do the work – work the Word. The Word gives us the power to crucify those ungodly thoughts in the name of Jesus. When an idea or thought comes to mind, take a moment and ponder. Ask yourself, "Who sent this thought?" The thoughts of God are righteous. So, if that thought is overwhelmingly negative, it is not from God.

We find self-confidence in this:

> I will give you the keys of the kingdom of heaven;
> whatever you bind on earth will be bound in heaven,
> and whatever you loose on earth will be[b] loosed in
> heaven. (Matthew 16:19 NIV)

Believers have been given kingdom access. We have the power to free our minds! We can decree and declare, which means coming to a conclusion that those thoughts are bound in the name of Jesus. We can release peace, mental stability, and clarity in the place of confusion and worry. We declare by the power of the Word that we are free of negativity. Our minds are renewed and strengthened, and our freedom is settled in heaven. Positivity is from heaven and negativity is bound on the earth. We are free!

Change the channel in your mindset. Don't rehearse the negative. It's a trick to keep you trapped.

Words of Life

I praise You Father for a new day. I am mentally free by the power of Your Word. I am delivered from thinking negative thoughts from the enemy. I thank You that You are my source of peace. Your Word gives me the wisdom to combat the voices of the enemy. I decree and declare that I will speak Your Word in authority to silence the evil voices. Daily, I will use my spiritual keys to bind the enemy when he comes against me. Through faith, I have the mind of Christ; therefore, I walk in victory being mentally tough with a champion state of mind.

The Challenge

How can you take control of your thoughts? What does it mean to be transformed by the renewing of your mind, according to Romans 12:2? Explain.

Write a confession to defeat the enemy in your mind. Read and meditate on it daily.

I'M RIGHT. THEY'RE WRONG

I'm sure we have all been in situations where we felt we were right about something. However, in pursuit of being accurate, an unnecessary argument ensued. We desire to be right but what's more important to God is that we are righteous.

The Message

"They're wrong, and I'm right." How many times have you heard this statement? It's so easy to get caught up in the right and wrong dilemma. My dad was a very wise man. When I was young, he taught me to be careful not to fight wrong so hard that you become wrong. That is something to think about, isn't it? As saints of God, coming to a righteous resolve is the principle thing. If we're not careful, we can be so adamant about being right that we inadvertently move God out of the picture altogether. Have you ever met someone who always had to be right? To them, being right was all that mattered; it was worth gold.

Be careful not to fight wrong so hard that you become wrong.

At times in my life, I placed such a high value on being right that I failed to realize God was not in my rightness. God already knew. He saw it, and He heard it all. My thoughts were not new to Him. Thank God for self-evaluation and growth! Listen. The situation you were upset about was not that serious. There was no need to go that far in pleading your case. God invites us – He waits for us – to let things go so He can bless us unimaginably.

Have you ever been in a situation and knew God was instructing you to leave it alone? Did you know deep inside He wanted you to let Him be your vindicator? You were convinced of this but somehow, you could not shake it; you couldn't get over it, You just *had* to continue until you were satisfied that you got your point across. You had to prove you were right. Friend, the blessing you were praying for was essentially held up because of your persistence to strife. I've been there. I've climbed that mountain before and learned many lessons. The flesh wants to be right. The flesh insists on being right. God desires that we pursue righteousness, not the desire to be right. Pursuing (chasing) God's righteousness determines our blessings and our gifts from Him. God has so many great things in store for us. However, He is waiting for some of us to get over our right to be right. Let it go; you will feel better. You will.

Here's the remedy. Put your flesh under arrest and hand it over to God. He is the righteous Judge. He is fair and will judge and adjust accordingly. We hold grudges, and we refuse to forgive because what happened to us happened. It is undeniable. It happened. Furthermore, when it happened, it was their fault. It was all them. Maybe you feel justified to carry the hurt and pain because you didn't deserve it in the first place. So, you speak about it. You dwell on it. You feast on it. You sleep on it. You awake to it.

Consumed with being right at any cost will cause you to be full of self and selfishness. Being in the flesh will take you out of the will of God if you are not careful. Process that and think about it. Selah. Many fight hard to keep their reputation. They continuously fight at all costs to expose and dismantle a lie, which was not worth the fight or stress in the first place. Whose approval are we searching for? Whose matters? Vengeance belongs to the Lord.

> Dearly beloved, avenge not yourselves, but rather give
> place unto wrath: for it is written, Vengeance is mine;
> I will repay, saith the Lord (Romans 12:19).

Fight hard to be right with Christ. He is the greatest example of a person who chose not to fight to be right. The proof came later; when it came, it was beautiful and glorious. We must strive to be like Christ. In doing so, we are better, not bitter. Being like Him should be our primary focus. Justification is a nasty distraction that consumes valuable time and energy.

If we are not healed, repeatedly talking about what we have been through and holding on to it gets us nowhere. Nowhere. It pushes us deeper into bitterness and pollutes others in the process. We ignorantly pull others – innocent to our greed and stubbornness – into our obsession to be right. Let righteousness and righteousness alone be your victory.

Words of Life

Father, I honor You for You are holy. I choose to fix my eyes on You. I surrender my will to You, and I will walk in Your righteousness. Thank You for forgiving me when I walked in the flesh and insisted on being right. Thank You for liberation. I submit my mind and my emotions to You. I commit to focusing on Your Word, and I will speak Your truth, rather than my opinions.

The Challenge

What have you passionately sought to be right about and how did it affect your life?

What might you consider doing differently should you experience this situation again?

PROVERB NINE
GOD'S
PEACE

What is peace? Is peace holding my tongue when I want to respond in anger? Is peace giving up the right to avenge or seek revenge? Is peace being quiet when asked to give a reason for my true feelings? Is peace trusting in God for the answer and not searching for peace in my intellect? How can I truly experience peace?

The Message

Peace. My stabilizer. Without God's peace, many would go crazy. I know I would. Have you ever been in a situation that led you to cry out to the Lord for peace of mind? Have you ever said to yourself, "If I could just get a little peace in this situation, I'd be OK"? What does it mean to truly be at peace? You've totally surrendered all worries, concerns, pain, and discomfort when you receive the peace that only God can give. You have given it all to the One in control.

Without peace, there is no way we can make it. No, we might make it, but how would the road to "making it" be? Life would be complicated – even more so than it is now. We've all been there. Life presents a multitude of tests (some harder than others) to face, conquer, and defeat. Without God's peace, our minds would be overloaded with unrest. Peace is a sweet friend – the type of friend you miss when he/she is away. Peace is the type of friend only found through Jesus. "What a friend we have in Jesus." Do you remember that old, sweet hymn sung by grandmothers and grandfathers?

I've worked in social services for many years. Many times, I've walked the halls of mental health units witnessing people – young and old – frantic, dazed, paranoid, and in the midst of delusions. Sometimes, they were so out of it that they disregarded everyone, even those trying to help them, as a threat to their safety. They were in survival mode and fighting (physically and sometimes emotionally) was their outlet. They would withdraw and become guarded. Mentally, they were completely removed from their surroundings. No peace. In isolation – a famous design of the enemy. Without peace, our minds are vulnerable to the enemy's tactics.

I vividly recall a day on the job when I encountered a gentleman who had lost so much of himself, so much of his mind; he didn't know where he was. He was a middle-aged man, and when I met him, he was lying in the corner of his unit. He had pulled himself into a fetal position, and his face was toward the ground. The little I learned about him that day was astonishing. He was an intelligent man with two master's degrees. He had a mind filled with incredible knowledge and facts but sadly, his mind and his peace were gone. He lost his ability to cope. He checked out of life. He was prescribed psychotropic medications to help him sleep and to close out the voices that permeated his mind and stole his peace. He was diagnosed as clinically depressed. Regularly, he became overwhelmed with unrest. During those times, I was reminded how blessed it is to experience the peace of God.

What happened to him? What caused this dissension? If we are true to ourselves, it makes sense to say, "Life happened." That's it. Life. See, if you are breathing, you too can testify that life has a way of sending challenges your way. Maybe he lost the ability to cope with life's stressors. Maybe it all became too much to handle. Have you been there? Yeah, me too. Life can become difficult at times. Checking out seems to be the best and most logical choice when life throws a sucker punch. It can get really tough. The weight of life can become too much to bear. It is a fact that some of us are one bad decision from being in a similar situation. No peace.

Many of us are mentally stable, per se, because we still have the ability to deal with difficult situations effectively. Thank you, Jesus! We've learned how to carry on when things go awry or maybe we were born with such ability. Whatever the case, it's there. It holds us together when things around us fall apart.

I can easily flashback to my life when I first became a pastor's wife. I was not ready for the journey at all. I was arguing with God. Totally. My husband was ready for the mission. I was stuck in my thoughts – full of hesitation, doubt and what I know to be resentment. "You're really going to do this... really? Are you sure?"

See, I had my own plans. I was trying to travel and enjoyed having no responsibilities. Then reality hit. My husband took over the pastorship of my late father-in-law's church, Greater Evangelist Temple. My husband honored and accepted his father's decision to take over his church. He told me, "I'll take on the work for a short while." The church was comprised primarily of family and a good number of faithful members. Though challenging, it was not hard to settle in and make ourselves at home. We grew as people and as leaders. The church grew, and souls were saved. We learned a lot about the many facets of ministry and people.

Two years came and went so very quickly. My husband came home one day, seemingly out of the blue, and said: "Dear, the Lord told me it's time to move on, leave my dad's work, and build a Greater Harvest."

"Excuse me? What? You can't do that!" I'm one to speak my mind, so I was quick to tell him what I thought.

His response to me was, "I must be obedient to God."

I wrestled with his decision. I just could not wrap my mind around us leaving. I couldn't find rest when I tried to sleep at night. Talk about torment! What would people say or think? How would I say goodbye? What about what we started? I was mad, sad, and frustrated all at the same time. I couldn't talk him out of it (and I tried a couple of times), for it was a kingdom agenda. The torment became heavier and stronger for me when people started asking questions. I felt the need to give the response I thought they wanted to hear. Some thought we were outside the will of God and promoting our own agenda. We faced judgment and ridicule at so many different levels from the saints – the very people we prayed for. A pastor, one we loved and supported, told us we would be cursed. Jesus! Yes, cursed. Of course, we didn't receive those words.

I learned a lot about my husband during that time. Actually, what I saw in him reinforced what I already knew about him. His strength and faith were bold, and I found refuge in watching how he handled it all. He did not say a word to defend himself although it was disheartening. While he fought in peace, humility, and assurance of God's will, my peace had been stolen. I was the First Lady – yes, but I did not know how to fight that fight. I can look back at that time now and say I had no wisdom. It had not been developed. It was all too fresh for me. I watched my mother, also a pastor's wife, handle such situations. However, I was never exposed to anything like this before. I had never witnessed this side of the church.

I remember riding by the bluffs one night. There, I saw a deep drop in between two of the hills. I entertained the thought of driving my car over the cliff – just to get some semblance of peace. Maybe if I took too many pills, I'd find peace. I felt as if my only way to be at peace was to disconnect from the situation that was draining me of every ounce of sanity I was desperately holding onto.

I remember lying on the floor in my den crying. My daughter, Alexis, was young then, maybe seven years old or so. She approached me innocently and said, "Mom, you have to let whatever it is go." Then, she read Psalm 23 to me. You'd think that was enough to turn things around for me, but it wasn't. I had adopted a victim spirit. I was trying to please God, my husband, and people, all at the same time. Impossible. I still had no peace. During this time, I learned something about myself. I loved deeply and too hard to a point where I was trying to please everyone. I also learned people love differently. I allowed my emotions to override my spirit. Emotions can become risky if not checked, for our emotions do not always authenticate reality.

> *Emotions can become risky if not checked, for our emotions do not always authenticate reality.*

The enemy works hard at replacing reality with perception. He is cunning and slick. He will make you think what's happening in your world is a personal attack on your emotions and intelligence, when, in reality, the storm is kingdom based. I will never forget, one day while in a beauty shop, a sister saint approached me and said, "I heard y'all left and took all the members." I didn't know what to think. Nevertheless, I was blown away; probably because I was still wrestling with the idea of us leaving myself. I could not believe that she didn't recognize how fragile I was. I thought, "Can't you tell how this is impacting me? Where is your discernment?" I didn't see this, initially, but I now know I needed to be in my prayer closet, all along, in preparation for interactions like this.

By default, I was the First Lady. I had to follow my husband in obedience to God, but I was having a hard time. I wanted – no, I needed – the saints, women of God, to embrace and support me with encouragement.

I craved it! Thank God for a praying mother who encouraged me to stay focused, especially during this time in my life. She reminded me that the outcome would be the testimony – my testimony. I wanted peace. I desired it. I could taste it. I longed for it, but I didn't know how to pursue it. Of course, I had the Word of God. I knew the scriptures, but my peace was shaken and shifted by my circumstances.

My husband decided to be a pastor, but I was suffering from his decision. That's where I was mentally at that time. Not to mention, the enemy monopolized my hurt. His plan was to discourage me so I could discourage my husband. What a lesson to learn. I learned that the enemy worked hard to set me up and though hard to admit, at times, he was winning. He was actually winning, and I was allowing him to. The strategic plan of the devil was to rob my peace, so I would not have the fight in me to stand for what the Lord had ordained.

I needed to change, and I knew why. I needed to heal. I was in this place of hurt too long. It was another one of the enemy's designs. I was trapped. I needed to be delivered from people and people's perceptions of me. I was tired of being defeated. I will never forget sitting in my living room, alone, asking God to deliver me from people. I cried out to Him! I told Him I desperately needed His peace, and I committed to serving Him.

My husband, my solid rock, had the peace I so desired. He was secure and confident in what God told him, and he was standing on God's Word. He fell so gracefully into God's plan. On the other hand, I had not yet realized God had a plan for me as well. I was too engrossed in hurt and disappointment. It was a distraction crafted specifically for me by the enemy.

Friends, I was so wrapped up in emotions, I told God, "Lord if you don't hear and help me, I'm going to start fighting the saints." Yes, I said it. Fighting! Funny thing was… back in the day before I was saved, I would fight and win, but in the church, I was a crybaby. The enemy wanted me to resort to the old man. He knew my triggers oh so well.

In the midst of my frustration, I found the strength to jolt back at the devil. "No, devil, I won't do it!" The truth was I still had no peace. I was confused and frustrated, but I was seeking peace. I knew it was available to me. I was broken but fighting for my peace. I was slandered by the people, but still fighting for my peace. My character was on trial while I was fighting for my peace. I told God about my concerns, and I pleaded my case. I needed peace. God did just what I asked Him to do… when I asked.

At that moment, I recognized yet another tactic of the enemy. Deception! Tricks! He is the architect of lies. He drafts, designs, and engineers things for us to fail. He made me take the long route to my deliverance, but God provides other options should we receive them.

God gave me peace when I stopped worrying. When I stopped justifying my position, talking about the situation, and committed to prayer, God worked it out. Vent up, not out. Vent to God or to someone God places on your heart. Vent to someone who can help guide you. I learned this lesson too many times. I get it now! I thank God, every day, for blessing my mind and strengthening my will to fight for my peace. The old but true saying: "If you hold your peace and let the Lord fight your battle, victory shall be yours." Victory prevailed for me, and it will prevail for you too. While on this journey called life, we must have God's peace.

> These things I have spoken unto you, that in me ye might have peace. In the world he shall have tribulation: but be of good cheer; I have overcome the world (John 16:33).

Jesus. He has overcome this world, and He alone gives us peace. We can rest safely in our salvation and stand firm in the words of our Savior. Our ability to remain solid and mentally stout in this life depends on God's peace. His peace is our sanity. It stabilizes life's problems.

His peace is our sanity. It stabilizes life's problems.

We must be confident in this:

> And the peace of God, which passeth all understanding, shall keep your hearts and minds through Christ Jesus (Philippians 4:7).

We must take courage and anticipate the experience of God's peace. If by chance, you do not have God's peace, it may be that you're enduring a test. You may be under a calculated attack of the enemy. I know because I've been there.

We will experience problems without a detour but we must remember we serve a sovereign God of peace. In the words of Dr. Hart Ramsey, "Protect your peace. Satan uses the noise in your soul, situations, and surroundings to drown out the voice of God!" The blessing and the comfort come in knowing the Lord desires peace for us, and He freely gives it if we only ask.

Words of Life

Father, I thank You for peace. Your peace, Father, helps me balance my day. It gives me the mental capacity to take on challenges. I thank You that I can run to You to settle my mind when life gets heavy and unbearable. Peace is my possession. It's a gift from You. I appreciate the work You do behind the scenes perfecting all that concerns me. I can breathe. I can relax because You are my harmony. You are my calm in the face of trouble.

The Challenge

What have you allowed to steal your peace and caused you not to seek God?

What is the meaning of this passage of scripture? "Thou will keep him in perfect peace, whose mind is stayed on thee: because he trusteth in thee" (Isaiah 26:3).

PROVERB TEN
SISTERHOOD
a
VILLAGE

A village of women with mirrored values is hard to come by – women who accept the beauty life gives, along with its challenges. If you are hurting, a strong sisterhood will take on your hurt and help you carry the hurt. A village of women who invest time to help one another be better than yesterday. A village that is stronger than the past, more capable tomorrow, and powerful in its own right. Pure sisterhood – ready and willing to stand united and smart enough to know that more is accomplished this way. In God, we conquer all. There is no opposition. Well, maybe. And if so, we win.

The Message

Sisters, we must believe in the meaning, not just embellish how beautiful the word sounds. We speak it but don't mean it at times. Think about it. We call one another when we need something, but when we're OK, we disappear. Sisterhood should always be near – in good and bad times. One of my absolute favorite scriptures is this one:

> Iron sharpens iron, so a man sharpeneth the countenance
> of his friend (Proverbs 27:1).

We make one another better, stronger, and wiser. To be sharpened means to be joined and growing together to meet the challenges of life. Your development, growth, and in some cases, your healing, can only take place when you walk right and with the right women. You cannot partner successfully with someone who does not share your goals. When you feel passionate about something, but they do not, start watching; be careful, and activate discernment. Do not link up with sisters who don't share your God-given purpose. Do they support you and encourage you? Do they join you in celebration and sorrow?

When you feel passionate about something, but they do not, be careful, and activate discernment.

Link up with sisters who can sharpen you and give you the opportunity to sharpen areas of their lives. Enter a godly covenant with sisters who empower you, so that you may empower other women. We live in a time when women spend so much time being caddy, hating one another, and being envious of each other, instead of supporting and loving one another. This is such a harsh word. It's difficult to deliver it and difficult to receive it. However, I must be honest. When you encounter a sister who is not authentic, it is called being fake. Don't. Be. Fake. Or, you might be thinking, "Maybe they are not fake. Maybe this is just who they really are. Maybe they are just wired like this. Some people are just built like this." It still begs the question: why are they continuing to act out? They haven't changed, grown, improved, or elevated themselves as a person after all this time? We have all had to overcome something; yet, we're still fighting? When you truly think about it, it's quite unbelievable. I don't like the devil causing women to be at odds with one another. He is behind it all.

Celebrate your sisters! We are all beautiful, fabulous, and gifted. Psalm 139:14 affirms, "I am fearfully and wonderfully made: marvelous are thy works." This is me, and this is you! God made you to look like me and me to look like you. God made us special sisters. He took His time creating us, and in creation, He knitted us with a special bond. There is no space for jealousy. Ain't nobody got time or energy for drama. We should all be capable of operating maturely and respectfully. That's behavior fashioned by God. The sisterhood has your best interest at heart; it catapults you to the next level. If you get to the top before your sister does, she's not mad or bitter. She does not question her capabilities; she celebrates with you until it is her turn to be celebrated. Covenant with the sister who will pray, cry, laugh, and rejoice with you during all times of your life. In turn, do the same for her.

I am so grateful God blessed me with amazing and powerful sisters who have been in my life for over 35 years. We love each other. Since elementary school, God has been shaping the sisterhood by way of our upbringings and the teachings of our parents and grandparents. Values start in the home. We were shown how to love for real for real y'all. Real love. Love is something you experience heart to heart with each other. When one was hurt, we all were hurt. When one of us fought, we all fought and were determined to win. If we didn't win, we came back the next day for a new round. If someone came for one, he came for us all. Period. You have no idea how deep we are – still strong and still standing. Thank God we're saved and sanctified now – we're fighting for Jesus!

Within our sisterhood, we searched for solutions to problems together while in prayer. We waited for God's answers. Sisterhood! Even if we argued to get it right, we did it together. Conference calls were necessary at times to make sure our unit was secure, and group text messages were, and still are, our thing! We're not perfect, but we are strong in our bond. We've learned that our relationship is not only for us. It is for young ladies coming behind us who are yearning for living examples of sisterly love. We pray that they, too, will learn the value of sisterhood and what it represents. Though our circle started out fairly small, each of us made friends outside of our sisterhood and introduced them to the love we have for each other. Our circle enlarged, and this was a beautiful thing!

There was, and still is, no competition, envy or fault-finding, only admiration. We stood constant and solid, and we all celebrate one another while embracing the low points and sad days. When we had to bear the sorrow of a sister and attend the funeral of her loved one, we took up an entire row! We mourned and conquered together. Our children belonged to every one of us. As mothers, we offered the same support and love. It takes a village! Our husbands became friends themselves, and they are all supporters of our sisterhood. We travel, dine, and often laugh, so much so, we cry! We understand what sisterhood means, and we fought throughout the years to remain a unit. Sisterhood's value is priceless. It's so worth fighting for!

A little advice: don't give your sisterhood to the enemy for our young ladies to see us fail. We can't do that! They are watching us. We are their examples;

therefore, we must fight to keep what God loves – unity. We must be better than statistics. All women don't fall out of love, hate, stir up confusion, and throw knives. All women don't have two faces and behave like chameleons changing their colors instantly. Please, ladies, stand and stop changing your colors! God is not in that. Remain true, honest, and real with each other. Stay solid! Don't pretend! It's called integrity!

We are forever thankful to God for our aunties, big sisters, and sisters-in-love for their wisdom, mentorship, and push to make us better. We accepted instruction and appreciated the long talks and constructive criticisms. We did not – and still don't – take it for granted. What they taught us instilled tremendous blessings in our young lives. It mattered then, and it matters now. Sisterhood. The irreplaceable village. When you have the opportunity to experience it, receive it and hold it close, its value is priceless.

Words of Life

Father, I thank You for my sisters and the love You placed within us. Sisterhood is beautiful, empowering, and a necessity. This unbreakable bond is precious and dear to the heart. I thank You, for You created us to be examples of love. We are remarkable expressions of who You are. Father, I will continue to trust You with us. Every good thing comes from You, and this is good. I pray that this reader find a sisterhood – or brotherhood – to support them through every trial and triumph. Teach us all to be great sisters and brothers.

The Challenge

What are some of the challenges you have faced with sisterhood or have witnessed that create conflict among women? Explain.

Do you believe sisterhood is necessary? Why or why not?

PROVERB ELEVEN

A CONSTANT FRIEND

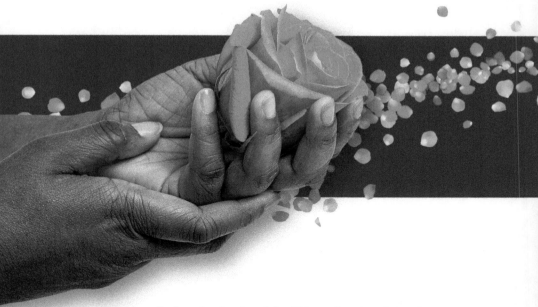

So close, we feel each other's spirit. Although going through, we are never changing because we care. When I'm quiet, she's praying because she knows that is what I need at that moment. She is constant, even in quietness. Constant in pressure. Constant when others see differently. The friendship never changes. I got you, and you got me. We have no time to judge because we both know there's just too much work to do. The heart is clearly seen, and the heart is faithful.

The Message

The ultimate example of friendship is the story of Ruth and Naomi. Ruth lovingly said:

> Entreat me not to leave thee, or to return from following after thee: Wherever you go, I will go; wherever you live, I will live. Your people will be my people, and your God will be my God. Wherever you die, I will die, and there I will be buried. May the Lord punish me severely if I allow anything but death to separate us (Ruth 1:16-17).

Naomi was an Israelite woman. During a time of famine, she and her family relocated to the country of Moab. Sadly, her husband Elimelech and two sons Mahlon and Chilion, died while in Moab. She decided to return to her hometown. She had two daughters-in-law, Ruth and Orpah; all three women were now widows. Naomi tried her best to discourage Ruth and Orpah from returning home with her. She advised them to go back home because she had nothing left to give them. Orpah kissed her mother-in-law goodbye, but Ruth refused to leave Naomi. She returned to Naomi's hometown with her.

The story of Ruth and Naomi is about love and friendship, but it's also about the pain and grief these women shared and experienced together. They'd lost their husbands; each of them had experienced loss. They understood each other's heartbeat because they had suffered the terrible misfortune of death together. Ruth had a tight bond with Naomi. To leave her was not an option. She loved Naomi; she believed in her. Their relationship and bond were constant and unshakeable. Real!

Have you experienced a friendship like this? One that is founded on love and respect. Do you have a true friend who has stuck it out with you against all the odds? Did your friend remain unmoved and unshaken when you were surrounded and pressured? It's important to know who you're rolling with! Know who is by your side! Know who's got your back. What's their pedigree? Do they have the right spirit?

What character traits do they possess? Are they constant and faithful? Do they have the strength to help you stand in peaceful times, as well as times of adversity? Friendship takes a lot of work. I know. However, the sacrifice is worth it. Try harder.

Naomi realized Ruth's determination to go with her. Their relationship wasn't a surface relationship. What's a surface relationship? One that does not possess the strength to withstand anything deeper than a surface cut. Simple. Weak. The love Naomi and Ruth had for each other had deep roots that transcended age, hurt, and the mutual pain they shared.

Nothing could destroy the bond that Naomi and Ruth had. Not an argument. Not money. Let them have it. Not a lie. Don't chase the lie. Not hearsay. Did you hear it with your own ears? If so, let's talk about it – have a conversation. Not gossip. The enemy gets a kick out of women gossiping. Not a man. He's not worth it; there's another woman or two besides you. Not envy. Ladies, don't covet your friend's stuff. God has yours, so wait your turn. Not strife. It's not that serious, really… forgive. Not jealousy. We are all beautiful, talented, and special.

Jealousy is as cruel as the grave. The O'Jays said, "They smile in your face. All the time they want to take your place. The backstabbers." And lastly, don't let past issues separate you. Deal with your heart's posture and let it go. How long does one ponder on letting go before actually letting go? Too long. Let nothing separate you! That's the part women really must get. A constant friend will tell you the truth despite your discomfort, and in turn, cause you to become a better you.

> *A constant friend will tell you the truth despite your discomfort and cause you to become a better you.*

> Faithful are the wounds of a friend; but the kisses of
> an enemy are deceitful (Proverbs 27:6).

A true friend will tell you the truth even when it hurts. She will tell you the "honest-to-God" truth when you're at fault, out of line, or when you're about to make a poor decision. Honestly, as women, we don't tell each other the truth as we should because we don't want to deal with conflict. Or, we just don't know how to deal with it properly. A constant friend will pull out the best in you in love and truth even when you're at your worst. A constant friend will hold you up when you are broken and lifeless and encourage you to hold on. I'm talking about that God-given friend who will intercede on your behalf and through the pureness of their prayers, blessings are released.

Ruth and Naomi's relationship was strong and sustainable because they'd experienced so much together. Unlike some women, they were tight. They stuck together. Think about it. Sometimes when we get more, we forget. When we don't want to be bothered, we don't answer the phone; we are quick to send the call to voicemail. I get it; however, love picks up that phone after the third message. It's respect. It's understanding. A constant friend loves all the time, not only when it benefits them or is convenient. We pretend we're not at home when we hear that knock on the door. I understand that part too; alone time is good. However, maybe that friend needs your listening ear and your shoulder to cry on. Sometimes – many times – friendship isn't about you. Rather, it's about the mutual needs each of you has and the support you can give to each other. Friendship comes from God. God gave that person to you. He gave you someone to complement you, someone who would be in your corner when others abandoned you. How sad that we forget at times.

God wants us, women, to be delivered from the spirit of moodiness. Sacrifice yourself. Unfortunately, some of us forget we've not always lived like we're living now. Ladies, we come from the same neighborhood and the same schools. We walked to school together; we played on the swings and in the mud together. We shared each other's clothes. Now, we're educated and working in profitable careers, so we easily forget. Think about it. You have a man now, so there's no time to see how your sister is doing. But when you were broke naturally and bankrupt in your spirit, that one friend was there in the trenches with you, praying and interceding on your behalf.

I'm not saying you should be a hostage or a slave to that friend or any friend for that matter. Through prayer, God reveals and exposes those friends He wants us to release. I'm not saying give *all* your time to others and have no time for yourself. Just remember the impact of friendship in your life and let God direct you on how to be a good friend in return. Some of us just aren't good friends. Ask yourself this question, "Am I a good friend?" Maybe you need to rethink your definition of friendship. It can be difficult to be good to someone when you are not good to yourself. Is there mutual respect, encouragement, and support? What are you getting and giving in the relationship? Have a conversation. Know the position of your sister.

Heartfelt questions to ask:

♥ Do you consider me your friend?

♥ Are we close?

♥ Will you defend me?

♥ Will you tell me the truth even if it hurts?

♥ Will you cover me (in prayer)?

♥ Am I an asset or a liability?

♥ Are we standing with each other or what?

Be clear on where you stand and let nothing separate you. Nothing!

While Naomi was going through the difficult loss of her husband and two sons, I can imagine people on the sidelines watching her life. I imagine them thinking, "Naomi, are you that strong? Are you returning home with nothing? You left full, and you are returning home empty? Empty! Your husband is gone; your covering is gone; your sons are gone; you have no grandchildren, and others are watching you. Are you still going back home?"

Naomi thought she was returning home empty, but Ruth saw her returning home wealthy. She was wealthy in experience and wisdom. Ruth witnessed Naomi's experiences and in doing so, saw her strength and tenacity. You see what people are made of when they go through trials. It's during trials and tribulations that friendships mean the most.

> *It's during trials and tribulations that friendships mean the most.*

A constant friend will labor with and believe in you when you can't believe in yourself. She remains constant, stands close, and is never distant in her heart. Did you get the "never distant in her heart" part? At times, friendships can become distant because of life. It's not personal; the posture of the heart has not changed, but life has simply taken the lead. This happens. Life happens. When your relationship gets in this predicament, don't let the enemy settle in and place a wedge. Prayer uproots the thoughts that the enemy downloads in your mind. In prayer, there is no confusion and no misunderstandings, just quietness. We all know solace is needed at times. It is during this time that God can do His work.

I am blessed with constant friends who've been incredibly faithful to me. I recall the time when my father was transitioning from earth to glory. Others were there with me at his bedside: my sisters-in-love (strong in prayer and faith), Geneva, Helen, and my niece, DeAundra. We stood together, shaking, and crying. While waiting for my dad to take his last breath, we sang and read the Bible to him (Psalms 91) ministering to his spirit as he was transitioning. It was such a precious moment. It was glorious. No one left me. Even through the uncomfortable feelings of anxiety, pain, and hurt, we stood constant, and celebrated my dad's life, together. As my dad was transitioning, my friend Deanna was on the phone praising God, telling me to praise the Lord for my father's great life. My girlfriends Regina and Stacey soon arrived at the hospital providing emotional support. They wept with me while ensuring I was OK. Even through the hard reality of death, they were there. Constant. Steadfast.

Not too long ago, my daughter, Alexandria, had thyroid surgery. She was fearless and full of faith. She's my teacher. I witnessed her tenacity. God's grace carried her. As we were approaching the last hour, we expected to be in the waiting room. We settled there together as a family awaiting her prognosis. I was nervous and incredibly anxious. My friend, Marika, was there with me, prompting me to breathe, taking me on walks, and encouraging me to relax. As the doctor gave the unexpected diagnosis, I nearly buckled to the floor – an unexpected result, but our great God is so faithful. God is a healer. Thank you, Jesus! Marika was my strength. She said loudly with confidence, "Stand up. Listen to the surgeon. Alex will be just fine." As Ruth and Naomi were constant, a constant friend is there when you have no mental strength. They become your strength; they are incredible gifts to your life.

Words of Life

Father, thank You for constant friends. You have blessed us with wonderful and faithful friends who've helped us to believe in ourselves. God, we thank You that our hearts were open to friendship, and You placed special people in our lives to love and handle us as You do. We bless You today, and always for this love. Lord, help us continue to cultivate God-given relationships and treat others as Your Word instructs us. Thank You, Lord, for mutual respect and support for one another.

The Challenge

These days, are constant friends hard to find? Are good friendships hard to cultivate? Explain the reasons why and explore ways you can be part of the solution.

PROVERB TWELVE
LAUGH
in his
FACE

L aughter is good for the soul. It rids us of worry and stress even if just for a moment. It forces us to push through feelings we might associate with crying. It feels good. It's cleansing. It's the truth. The medicine of laughter has a healing power that warms the soul and is welcoming to a broken heart.

The Message

Have you ever taken a minute to reflect on your life and how good God has been? No, really, have you ever? I've sincerely reflected many times and asked myself, "How in the world did I get through all of that stuff?" God has brought me out of some ridiculously crazy and embarrassing moments. So much so that I know, without a doubt, He loves me! Have you ever reflected on your childhood and teenage years and considered the experiences you encountered that your parents – to this day – know nothing about? If we are honest and put all our cards on the table, we would have to face the truth – some of us could have been in jail. Some of us were caught stealing, smoking weed, drinking so much at a party we still don't know how we made it home. Some were almost kicked out of school but still graduated. It is the grace of God! Let's not forget about all the secrets of our past. Detrimental closet stuff. God covered you.

Think back – but for His glorious twins, Grace and Mercy, where would we be? It's easy to laugh to keep from crying when you realize if God didn't do it, you would probably still be stuck trying to figure out your deliverance. I remember all the times God bailed me out. Oh, how often we take those bailouts for granted! Yes, we do! Stop and consider the facts. In retrospect, it is God, not us, who introduced us to deliverance. Thank God for that introduction.

Bakersfield, California. South High School. Senior year. Graduation week. A risky combination! My girlfriends and I decided to turn the outdoor track at South High School into a speed raceway. Yep, we did. And here's the kicker: we were Drillers – Bakersfield High School Drillers. South High was our rival! We drove one of our cars on the track during track practice. Oh, yes! We were having a great time! We were laughing hysterically, hanging out the windows and hollering like we had no home training, "May the force be with you!" It was fun then – super fun. But that fun shifted to fear five minutes later when the principal locked the gate to the field. We were locked in. Yep. Locked on the track. Pure foolishness.

The principal was contacted, and we were nearly expelled but for God's grace and mercy. Other parents were called, but interestingly enough, my parents were never contacted. I don't know how that happened.

I didn't ask questions, and I just rolled with it. Somehow, my parents missed the call, and I was (and still am) completely OK with that! In fact, my mother never knew until after reading this chapter!

I've laughed and laughed over and over again just thinking about how God so mercifully rescues us out of situations we bring on ourselves. Self-sabotage is a killer we often fail to recognize, but it exists, and it's deadly. Take a moment to reflect. God is good, yes, He is. God is the antidote for our recklessness. Often, when we don't know what to do, He delivers us anyway (I had to take a deep breath right here). Thank You, Jesus, for deliverance.

> *Self-sabotage is a killer we often fail to recognize.*

I vividly remember another experience during my time in college. Lakeview was the street to ride down on weekends – the place to be. Lakeview Avenue was always on – any time of the day or night. You'd find people partying in cliques, hanging out, just having a good time. You would also see active drug deals, gangs, and interactions that didn't look too friendly. One weekend, my girlfriends and I decided to roll down Lakeview seven deep – Marika, Stacey, Regina, DeeDee, Shawn, and Tonia – windows down, music blasting, and yelling out the window – again, like we had no home training. Truthfully, we were just young and didn't consider the consequences of this decision. It was definitely a dangerous one. While riding, gunshots were fired, and our car shut down in the middle of the street! We were stuck. Couldn't move. Thank God for His divine protection! We were covered in the blood of Jesus! The car eventually started, and we laughed all the way home thanking God we didn't get hit by a bullet.

I didn't recognize it then, but our laughter was that of relief. You know the type – that godly laugh that erupts from the gut when you're thankful – just thankful – to be alive. God had done it yet again. He kept us from danger seen and unseen. It wasn't fun then, but it's funny now that we clearly see the enemy's plan for our lives at that time, and God's will that it did not come to pass. We are still here. We are all alive.

When the enemy reminds you of your past and confronts you with events of yesterday, laugh knowing God has covered you. Reflection is powerful. It reminds us of what could have been. It is also God's way of reminding us of His power. The danger, my friend, is in rehearsing. When we rehearse and ruminate on the past, it can keep us stuck in the very place God wants to deliver us from. If you allow him to, the enemy will taunt you by rehearsing negative episodes of your life in your mind. He knows our downfalls and triggers. He knows the things you value. He has figured out what gets you down and makes you feel defeated. He calculates your every move. He studies us daily and declares war in our areas of weaknesses. What he fails to grasp is that we have the upper hand. Stop! Do not give the enemy anything else to work with. Outsmart him. Laugh in his face because you are a new person.

> Therefore if any man be in Christ, he is a new creature: old things are passed away; behold, all things are become new (2 Corinthians 5:17).

You are a new creature in Christ Jesus. Convince yourself with the Word of God; you are a giant in Christ Jesus. You must have a champion mindset. It starts in your mind. Mental toughness is necessary to fight the wiles of the enemy. Remember, you reflect to learn; however, you look ahead to succeed. Don't give the enemy an opportunity to keep you in bondage. You survived your past. You still have your voice. You are alive. The enemy will try to take your voice and silence you if you allow him. He silences you by constantly reminding you how you weren't good enough. He taunts you about the mistakes you made causing you to rehearse the facts. The facts don't mean anything to God; He forgives.

When you allow the enemy to play tricks with your mind, you will continue to self-sabotage by revisiting your past. Self-sabotage interferes with progress. It is a distinctive trick of the enemy. He wants to block you from moving to a future you. A better you. A victorious you. He works hard to make you relive your past as if it is your today. He wants it to be fresh to you every day, just like the smell of fresh leather. Do you get it? You must! Your past is old. It's dead. It's no longer. When it's hard to believe, friend, you have to speak to yourself. Remind yourself that it is over. Don't take the bait. Don't be silenced. Open your big mouth and laugh at him. Laugh right in his face!

> *When you allow the enemy to play tricks with your mind, you will continue to self-sabotage by revisiting your past.*

Sometimes this effort might be painful. I know it sounds contradictory, but you might find it difficult to leave the old you behind. It might feel comfortable staying in the past because you've grown to believe what the enemy has fed to your mind. You have grown to accept his story as your story. He regularly reminds you of the embarrassments, hurt, pain and disappointments you once experienced to keep you in bondage. His goal is to enslave you to his devices. Strongholds. You must become stronger than that which binds you. Beware, for he presents you with a mirror – a reflection of who you once were and the person you may still believe you are. Don't accept it. Reject it! There are negative consequences if you accept. Shatter the mirror! Destroy it! Our God, the Creator of the universe, is an expert at making things new.

Change is hard. If you are having trouble getting past life's experiences, I encourage you to seek help. Having a person in your life who tells you the truth makes you accountable to your truth. One who stays in your face, and encourages you to make changes. Change is vital. Seek help from someone who has a strong set of values, good soil, and the strength and ability to help you keep out the negative weeds. Pull those tainted weeds out of your garden of success! Seek someone who will help you learn how to laugh – truly laugh – at the enemy.

A subject we often do not speak about in most churches is counseling. Why not? Counseling is not a forbidden thing but a necessary option at times. Everything is not a demon. Sometimes, people just need to be healed of past pain. Healed of old closet stuff. Healed of years of layers of the disappointment. Healed of unresolved issues. You can't get healed if you continue to conceal the wound.

I recall a time in my life when I would mask hurt. I would smile with those who caused me pain but return home and cry as I reminisced about the hurt of yesterday. The hurt, although old, was still fresh because I had not processed it. You can't heal what you won't express. I was holding on to that unexpressed hurt and wearing it as a hidden medal. A reminder from the enemy. It was my huge secret behind my smile and laughter. I'll never forget the day I told a friend, Rashonda, "They didn't see me crying." Her response was, "but you know you cried." She put my reality, my truth in my face. I was running from my reality as if I was OK. Lies. It was life-changing. I could no longer remain in denial. Wow! I was suppressing my hurt by masking it.

See, you smile, but smiles can be complicated when you are hiding from your truth. We laugh and pretend at the same time. Has this ever been you? You fear telling anyone because it may sound senseless, so you suppress your feelings. You bury them. You can't continue to suppress or even ignore the very thing that keeps you stuck in yesterday. As long as you continue to suppress, you can't progress. You deny yourself the ability to move forward. You deny yourself a victorious life. It's time to acknowledgment your pain by speaking your truth so you can live a greater life. I learned a powerful declaration made by Pastor Latanya Blake Allen, "It's a great day to live a greater life, and I'm living in my greater and I'm living in my future right now." See, if you don't let go, you can't live a greater life. God has a greater life and a brighter future for you when you release. That's the part we must get. By faith, you will get it, and you will be better than yesterday.

Some individuals get stuck in the process of their healing. They don't have the tools to effectively conquer the dark clouds that shrouded them and blocked life's sunshine for many years. Counseling helps you get to the root of the matter. It reveals why you remain stuck, trapped, and without deliverance. Expose your hurt to someone who is skilled to help you while not harming you. Someone who will not reach back later to use your pain and secrets against you. Effective therapy can help you navigate through your losses, pain, failures, and mistakes. It will get you to the finish line. Everybody needs a coach now and then. You need someone who will help you learn how to laugh from a place of freedom and true joy. A healed place. A place of wholeness.

You may never totally get over the pain of your past, but our great God will give you the grace to laugh and soar. Allow each test to help you evolve into the person God created you to be. He desires that we are healed, set free, and delivered in every area – mentally, psychologically, socially, and physically. This is your future! Laugh at the enemy and stop crying about yesterday. Let me encourage you with this passage of scripture:

And you hath he quickened, who were dead in trespasses and sins; Wherein in time past ye walked according to the course of this world, according to the prince of the power of the air, the spirit that now worketh in the children of disobedience: Among whom also we all had our conversation in times past in the lusts of our flesh, fulfilling the desires of the flesh and of the mind; and were by nature the children of wrath, even as others. But God, who is rich in mercy, for his great love wherewith he loved us, even when we were dead in sins, hath quickened us together with Christ, by grace ye are saved (Ephesians 2:1-5).

We are forgiven of our past. Completely. When the enemy rears his head and presents you with a picture of your yesterday, stop, smile, and laugh. It is a fact. He will not win. See yourself better until you believe it.

Words of Life

Father, thank You for Your grace and mercy. I trust You with my insecurities. You are the one who makes me smile when I am gloomy. Thank You for a long, beautiful life. Thank You for strengthening and empowering me to laugh at the enemy and his devices. I am the head and not the tail; he is beneath me. I am reminded of Proverbs 17:22, "A merry heart doeth good like a medicine: but a broken spirit drieth the bones." I am thankful that laughter is my strength. I will continue to laugh knowing You love me. Although I face the challenges of life, Lord, my heart is happy, and I rejoice, for You are my King. God, thank You for laughter, smiles, and kind eyes. Thank You for fun, friendships, and stress relief.

The Challenge

What experiences from your past has the enemy tried to hold you in bondage to? How long have you faced this plot?

Find a scripture that relates to the bondage you identified, and write your confession. Read your confession out loudly, each day, and learn to laugh.

PROVERB THIRTEEN

BEAUTY, BRAINS, *and* FAVOR

There comes a time in our lives when God tests us to see if we are willing to do what He asks. Our obedience is the gateway to His favor. It doesn't matter who we are, where we are from or our social or educational status. It doesn't matter how much money we make. None of these determine our levels of blessing, per se. It is by our obedience and God's unfathomable grace that we are tremendously blessed.

The Message

You may remember Esther from the Bible. I admire Esther because the grace and favor in her life were extraordinarily evident. Her obedience to God led to many blessings. Queen Esther was born a Jew named Hadassah. Her uncle, Mordecai, raised her and would later become her informant and teacher. In the first chapter of the book of Esther, the king, Ahasuerus, hosted a grand party during the Purim holiday. On the seventh day, he called for his wife, Queen Vashti, to show off her beauty. She refused. Enraged by her refusal, the king took away her title as queen. Today, we would say he divorced her.

The Bible tells us the king made this decision because of Vashti's disobedience and disrespect. You don't tell the king, "No". This behavior sent a negative message to the other women who were looking on. After the dismissal, the king immediately began his search for a new queen. He sent a decree throughout the land and asked that all the virgins be gathered. Esther was a virgin, but she had no desire to be a part of this process. However, her uncle, Mordecai, gave her instructions to follow the king's request and remain quiet. Out of obedience, she did just that.

> Esther had not yet shewed her kindred nor her people; as Mordecai had charged her: for Esther did the commandment of Mordecai, like as when she was brought up with him (Esther 2:20).

Esther respected Mordecai and trusted his direction. She was named queen and would later intercede on behalf of the Jewish people of the kingdom to save their lives. What a wonderful purpose!

What did God see in Esther? She had a genuine heart and an obedient spirit. She remained true to what she had been taught, and she was obedient to Mordecai. She believed he knew what was best for her. Esther didn't succumb to superficiality. That's what I love about her. Can you imagine the level of competition? It was one special lady's opportunity to be queen. Esther wasn't even competing.

Think about it. Are there times you feel the need to compete? If so, why? You don't have to fight for what's already yours when there's favor in your life. Esther knew where she came from – having nothing – yet, she also knew to whom she belonged. She wasn't caught up in the glory of becoming royal. Position, status or title didn't move her. In our world, it seems as if many people fight to be first but end up last. Is it worth the fight? Is it? Many focus on the glamour and tend to get caught up in wanting all eyes on them. Some need the attention in order to proclaim, "I'm winning." But, are you? Probably not. And you do not please God either. Our mission should be to please God first.

When purpose and destiny are calling you to a higher place, there's no time to be caught up in trying to get attention and seeking accolades. There's work to do, and it takes time! Esther had to go through to get where she was; it didn't come overnight. So it is with you. You can't get to the top overnight. Let God do it. Take your time or risk God giving someone else your turn – until you are ready. Are you ready? Wait for it. Don't faint. Wait to be processed by God! Allow the power of the Holy Ghost to shape and mold you. See, it's one thing to have beauty, but we need wisdom as well. Wisdom is the principal thing. We need brains for discernment.

For one year, Esther was made to go through a purification process, a cleansing. To be great in God, there is a process you will go through. It's inevitable. However, if you remain obedient to God, there is a blessing just for you on the other side of your obedience. Obedience is submission to God. If you let it, the very thing that tries to rob you of your life's desires will bless you.

At some point in our lives, God will allow situations to enter our world to teach us, make us think, mature us, and break us so we can have compassion for others. He will also do so to show us how to handle the flesh under pressure, and to push us forward. The book of Romans reassures us:

> All things work together for the good of those who love God and who are called according to His purpose (Romans 8:28).

The enemy works hard to interweave and knit dark threads through our lives. He mingles with important facets of our lives and works to integrate confusion to complicate our deliverance. Through his weaving, he even attempts to incorporate patterns to try and throw us off our spiritual path. Thank God, our God is bigger! It's cliché, but it's the truth: what the devil means for bad, God grabs, molds, and turns it around. He takes the good, the bad and the painful and shapes it for our good. That's a beautiful thing. The very thing that brought you pain – the set up that was meant to destroy you – was a promotion. It was a blessing in disguise! Think about it. It's working for your good.

Look at Esther's life. Promotion! God reveals His purpose through Esther's life. He worked through one obedient young woman to save the Jewish people from total annihilation at the hands of a forceful and powerful leader. Esther was beautiful, but she also had brains behind the beauty. She worked her faith. Esther appeared before the king on behalf of her people. I imagine her standing strong and proud. In my mind, I see her gazing into the king's eyes – intimidating as he was – capturing his heart, and finding his favor.

The king granted her rights and access to the kingdom. She was crowned queen. The hand of God was in her life. The king did not just see her beauty; he also saw the confidence behind it. Imagine Esther in your spiritual mind. She didn't flinch and tremble when she stood before the king. She was a confident woman in his presence although she was doing what had never been done before. She was unwaveringly confident in her God. She went before the king as an intercessor in efforts to save her people (the Jews) from being slain. It was against the law to appear before the king without permission; the penalty was death. She was prepared. Using her brains, she spoke with wisdom and authority giving her people instructions.

> Go, gather all the Jews who are present in Shushan, and fast for me; neither eat nor drink for three days, night or day. My maids and I will fast likewise. And so I will go to the king, which is against the law; and if I perish, I perish! (Esther 4:16 NKJV).

It appeared that Esther was on the verge of losing her life, but the favor of God stood with her. She was filled with determination. Before approaching the king, she asked the women to fast for her. She asked for support. Ladies, know the people who are part of your supporting cast. Are their lifestyles holy? Do they live with purpose and power?

Discernment is essential on your journey to success. Bear in mind that everybody is not praying for your good; rather, some are preying on you. Everybody is not excited about your success. Everybody does not wish you well, although they may say or act like they do. Some are not concerned about your victory. Not everyone has your best interest at heart. Look and take notice of the fruit people bear. Take heed. As my pastor teaches the congregation, "You can't let everybody sit on the front row of your life. Some people must reside in the balcony." It's OK to recognize that and act accordingly.

My girlfriend, Claudette, once told me, "You have to know where to file people." Are they supporters, takers, associates, friends, sisters or friendly enemies? It's important to know who the people in your life are and be real about it. Accept the truth as hard as it might be. It's hurtful. I know, but it's OK. The handmaids who prayed and fasted for Esther gave her strength to get the job done. Beauty, brains, and favor. When the king saw Esther standing in the court, she obtained favor in his sight; he extended his golden scepter to her. Without this gesture from the king, she would have died. However, at that moment, with faith, she touched the top of the scepter and made a connection with the king. I can see it; the connection she made with him was in the spiritual realm.

> Then the king said unto her, what wilt thou, Queen Esther? And what is thy request? It shall be even thee to the half of the kingdom (Esther 5:3).

Look at the favor of God! What is your request? What can I do for you? Name it. The king couldn't deny Esther because she walked in the presence of God. Confidently. God's glory walked before her. She walked in authority, wrapped in the Holy Ghost. At times in our lives, situations may appear bleak; facts may impede on our faith. Nevertheless, stand still and wait for God to work. There are blessings when we choose to be obedient. The Lord places us in positions to be used for His specific purposes. Esther's beauty and brains obtained favor from God.

Words of Life

Father, I thank You that favor surrounds me like a shield, and I am the apple of Your eye. I will continue to walk in the spirit of obedience and hold fast to the principles of Your Word. Father, I realize it is through obedience that You favor me, and I am made beautiful by You. I thank You for long life and godly wisdom. I will use that wisdom to teach and encourage others. I thank You, for I am made royal through You. Humbly, I come before You in submission. I embrace change, confident that You know what is best for my life.

The Challenge

Is there a task God has given you that you have not yet completed? If so, write it down. Evaluate the reason behind your disobedience or delay.

Write a declaration that will help you complete what God has instructed you to do.

Proverb Fourteen

IT'S
as CRUEL *as*
the GRAVE –
JEALOUSY

The largest audience rarely seen is the assembled spectators who oppose you. Haters or as some call them, frenemies, sit there at full attention watching and waiting for you to fall. The opposed – those jealous hearts – smile externally, but internally, something else simmers. Their strong desire for you to be defeated hides in a deep, dark chamber of their hearts. It's been there for so long that it has settled into the mind. Ugly, cruel, cold, and lonely. Happiness is an easier choice. Congratulating requires less energy. Complimenting seems fitting; yet, they are content to withhold the beauty of praise, not realizing their glow comes from your shine.

The Message

They admire from afar but refuse to praise. They hold on to jealousy, wanting what others have while failing to realize the beauty that exists in their world. They fail to realize that the spirit of hatred, fueled by jealousy, is a thief. It steals the gift of a simple compliment. Compliments have the potential to give someone else hope, life, and encouragement. What does one gain from jealousy? Nothing. It's important to call it what it is. Jealousy is a demon. It has a wicked presence while disguising as other emotions. It's a cold feeling. An enemy. A taker. Giving nothing but emptiness and taking away life. Have you ever met people who constantly speak of themselves, and refuse to see the good and successes of others? Have you ever brought this up to them, yet, they refused even to consider acknowledge it? Did they choose to deny ownership? Friend, please, don't be that person.

> *Jealousy is a demon. It has a wicked presence while disguising as other emotions.*

It's okay to praise and compliment someone else. In fact, it's encouraged and welcomed. We can all win. There are plenty of platinum platforms to go around. Another's success takes nothing away from you as a person. Choose to receive that! When you are unable to celebrate the successes of others, it's time to examine your heart. It's a heart issue.

Don't get comfortable with this spirit! Jealously is not of God! It's mean. Getting to the root of why jealousy has taken a seat in your life is vitally important. The inner voices that cheer on this destructive emotion must be silenced. The book of Solomon sends a profound message that all should heed:

> Set me as a seal upon thine heart, as a seal upon thine arm: for love is strong as death; jealousy is cruel as the grave: the coals thereof are coals of fire, which hath a most vehement flame (Solomon 8:6).

Like the grave, jealousy has shows no favoritism. It targets all ages, social statuses, genders and walks of life. It's grimy and causes us to act completely out of character. I heard someone say once, "Jealousy is the fear of losing something you believe is already yours." That's a complete lie from the enemy – a huge smokescreen. It's not yours; it does not belong to you. This is one of the enemy's most deceptive tricks – making you feel as if you're losing out on success when, in fact, it was designed specifically for someone else for this particular time. Jealousy will go a step further and make you believe it's someone else's problem when it's really yours. There is no life – no progress – when you walk in this spirit of jealousy. Jealousy keeps you stuck in time and prevents you from seeing miracles because it's the byproduct of fear.

Jealousy is simply negative energy wrapped in insecurities. It's a camouflage for the real issues. It's an evil, crippling energy that robs us of our spiritual walk. Ask yourself the real question, "Why are you jealous?" Do you want more of what someone else has? Is it confidence you need? Self-esteem? A career? Maybe a husband or family? If so, you can have it all. In time. You see, God blesses all of us; sometimes we just have to wait our turn. While waiting, it's important to take the time to praise others and celebrate with them. Sometimes, God is simply waiting for our hearts to get right. Addressing the heart issue is often the key to future favor. When jealousy is removed, life becomes full of peace, and you won't remain in pieces.

In *Othello*, Shakespeare said, "O beware of jealousy! It is the green-eyed monster that doth mock the meat it feeds upon." This spirit will cause your heart to be filled with evil devices and mischief. Jealousy breeds hatred, and hatred will make you act out of character. In the Bible, David and the armies of Israel were returning from the slaughter of the Philistines. It was common for the people to come out to the cities singing glorious songs and playing musical instruments with joy to meet the king. Although the people in the town were excited, Saul, on the other hand, was highly upset.

> When the men were returning home after David had killed the Philistine, the women came out from all the towns of Israel to meet King Saul with singing and dancing, with joyful songs and with timbrels and lyres. As they danced, they sang: "Saul has slain his thousands, and David his tens of thousands." Saul was very angry; this refrain displeased him greatly. "They have credited David with tens of thousands," he thought, "but me with only thousands. What more can he get but the kingdom?" And from that time on Saul kept a close eye on David (1 Samuel 18:6-9 NIV).

Look at jealousy in its grandness. Saul became angry and jealous; he felt threatened. He feared the kingdom would be taken from him. From that day forward, he looked at David with caution and made many attempts to destroy him. For example, in I Samuel 18:11, he threw a spear at him three times and missed. There were several instances when he plotted to have David killed by the Philistines. Jealousy will make you go to extremes. It took root in Saul's heart. Consequently, David's life was in danger. Here's the kicker: the anointing of God was on David's life, so jealousy could not kill him. Jealousy could not touch David. It was no challenge against the favor and protection of God.

Has this green-eyed serpent ever whispered in your ear? What did it say? What was your response? Jealousy will make you do all kinds of things in order to see others suffer – sometimes unto death. It is a destroyer of relationships and organizations. It has no boundaries and sees no kindness. This demon will destroy the very essence of a good thing, if we allow it. We must be in unity rather than against one another. We need this reminder at times. As people of God (the body of Christ), we must come together as one. Why?

> For as we have many members in one body, and all
> members have not the same office: So we being many,
> are one body in Christ, and everyone member's one
> of another (Romans 12:4-5).

This text equates the church of Christ to a human body. The members of the human body, your extremities, and internal organs neither exercise the same functions nor perform identical operations. Our bodies have many different parts; each one designed for a precise purpose, but all working in an organized manner to ensure the body keeps functioning. The result is synchronization, simply put. Togetherness. When a body functions as it is intended, the result is unity. We don't look the same, but we all have a purpose specifically designed for us. So why are we jealous of each other? God doesn't like it. It's senseless. We're all designed to do something different in and for the kingdom of God. The spiritual body, which is the redeemed of Christ, makes up but one body. It is a fact that we attend different denominations made up of many people, but we are one body in Christ Jesus. It has always been the will of God that we walk in love and unity with one another.

A unified body is necessary for us to increase in the things of God. As chosen sons and daughters, we must come together in one accord. Wholeness breaks through barriers and causes our God to move on our behalf. The miraculous manifests when we are whole. Illness, disease, infirmity, and strongholds are destroyed at the root. Putting aside jealousy, bitterness and other negative behavior naturally brings unity. Love is the antidote. We are reminded how love operates in the book of Romans, the law of love:

> Let love be without dissimulation. Abhor that which is
> evil; cleave to that which is good. Be kindly affectioned
> one to another with brotherly love; in honour preferring
> one another (Romans 12:9-10).

The scriptures encourage us to love without dissimulation. In other words, we must love without pretense, without masquerading or hiding true feelings, thoughts or intentions. Our love must be from pure hearts. God loves without hypocrisy. His love is sincere, true, and perfect. It's intentional. Scripture tells us to abhor that which is evil – reject it strongly! It means saying confidently and honestly, "No, I don't want to hear that about my sister or brother. I don't receive that." It means rejecting the negative. Before we speak, we must think. First Lady Mae Blake made this powerful statement: "Is it kind, true, or necessary?" Are your words kind and true? Was it even necessary for you to speak? Ponder on that.

The Word tells us to cleave, to draw close to that which is good. Godly love gives priority to others. Love is not jealous. It has no underlying motives, no other intentions. Love cancels out jealousy. Completely. Our gifts, talents, and offices are to build the kingdom effectively. We have to use these things to produce results and demonstrate excellence for the glory of God! Let's come together and attack this green-eyed spirit. Who is with me? We must move now. Now is the time.

Words of Life

My life is consumed by the law of love, and I am no longer held captive to jealousy. I am free. My heart is pure. As suggested in Ephesians 4:24, "I have put on a new man who is created in righteousness and true holiness." I love my brothers and sisters, and no evil flows from my lips or abides in my heart. I thank You, Father, that I have been given gifts and talents to share with others to edify God. I will continue to declare that jealousy has no place in my life. It is my enemy. I desire to be a beacon of love for Your glory.

The Challenge

How has jealousy manifested in your life? Explain.

Have you experienced jealousy? How did you overcome this spirit? If you struggle with jealousy, what steps will you take to get rid of it?

THE
CATALYST
of
PRIDE IS I

P ride is a spirit. A bold spirit. One that makes us feel as if we are above everyone and everything else. We hear no advice – no voice but that of our own. We look down, not to extend help or support, but to criticize. Simply put, pride somehow makes us forget where we came from – rags to riches. Remember that person back then? You. Since you've found it easy to forget who you were, think about what you needed back then. Someone had to help you at one time. Remember? Don't forget to remember. And be careful. Pride is a dangerous game.

The Message

Satan was all about the I. He was filled with it. He was kicked from heaven's domain because of it. He wanted to be above God.

Consider the I...

> How art thou fallen from heaven, O Lucifer, son of the morning, how art thou cut down to the ground, which didst weaken the nations! For thou hast said in thine heart, I will ascend into heaven; I will exalt my throne above the stars of God. I will sit also upon the mount of the congregation, in the sides of the north. I will ascend above the heights of the clouds; I will be like the most High. Yet thou shalt be brought down to hell, to the sides of the pit (Isaiah 14:12-15 emphasis added).

What happened to humility? Do you know it all? Do you have it all together? You don't. None of us do. Flawed. It's not about you and yours. It truly isn't. What makes you so special that you fail to appreciate the worth in others? It's time to do a self-check. Is this you? You are beautiful, eloquent, with a lovely smile, and gifted among many. Yet, the pride you walk in blocks all of these wonderful attributes.

We must all be reminded to continue walking in the spirit of humility. Humility breeds favor, and the favor of God surpasses everything. Humility takes you places and open doors for you. Without humility, your good attributes are invisible. They are buried under a heap of pride. Rather than seeing your beauty, others are faced with your pride and arrogance. I heard someone once say, "Pride exalts itself, excluding others, and loves revenge." Ugly!

It's pretty interesting when you think about it. Everyone can perceive pride in us, but us. Pride is a heart issue. Pride is not easily detected, especially when we're in denial. If we remain on our knees, God can show us what's in our hearts. If we fail to fast and pray against this ugly spirit, it can affect our vision and cripple us from seeing reality. Pride becomes a stronghold, and strongholds are hard to eliminate from our lives. A true fight ensues.

Everyone can perceive pride in us, but us.
Pride is a heart issue that's not easily detected.

The spirit of pride will cause you to sit on your praise when you know you need deliverance. Rather than praise, you worry about who is watching you. Pride will cause you to remain in pain and suffering when you know you need to be healed. You refuse to ask for prayer and help. Pride will keep you justified in being upset when God is pleading with you to let go. All along the way, this spirit continues to bury you further into spiritual death. It causes you to miss your blessings. It keeps you stuck in your feelings, rather than being interested in consulting God for truth. Humility is a strength; pride is a weakness. Pride says, "Look at me," while humility takes a back seat, for it is secure and confident.

Humble us, Jesus. When we don't tap into the spirit realm, we tend to miss the little, subtle things that go unnoticed. Pride is one of those things. Be careful. Pride can be very sneaky – showing up in ways you could never imagine. It's OK to apologize even if it's not your fault. Pride will keep you stuck in defending your stance. What does God love? He loves reconciliation and respect. Listen to others, just as they listen to you. Appreciate others just as they appreciate you. Pride refuses to change, while humility says, "I'll try."

I had to learn to listen when others spoke. My girlfriend Kimberly Watkin would tell me often, "Listen, Vicki. I need you to hear me. I need you to get it." I had to learn some things about healthy communication. Hearing and listening are two different things. Although we may hear someone speaking to us, we must listen carefully. Stop interrupting people when they speak. Let them complete their sentences. Humility pays attention, maintains eye contact and is engaged. Humility has a desire to learn. Pride cuts a person off when she is speaking and believes her own words are more important. People of God, stop being so confrontational, defensive, and adamant about making your haughtiness heard! When we think so highly of ourselves, we often become defensive of our status. Allow God to highlight you. Allow His glory to radiate, rather than working to pull others down to remain first. There is room for all of us to shine in Jesus!

Pride will cause you to miss the importance of another's words and focus on self. Pride is all about "me." If you have too much pride, it will become overwhelming and take over the godly spirit. We have to starve this flesh and feed our spirit man so that the ego can decrease. Honoring thyself and finding self-worth is a good thing. However, getting too much of a good thing can easily transition into a form of arrogance and conceit. Pride has the capacity to open doors that our human flesh cannot close. This can easily lead to a spiritual void and a complete disconnect with our heavenly Father. When pride causes our ties with God to be cut off, we begin to think we are our own by disregarding others and what they may have to say. Prideful human beings forsake humility and are condescending toward others in a shameless way. Saints, it comes down to making a decision: God or pride.

Pride is what caused the fallen state of humankind. Eve took it upon herself to disobey God's orders in the garden of Eden. Immediately, the world changed because of her prideful act. As it did with Eve, pride has the strength and audacity to open a window for Satan to creep into your life to kill and destroy. God despises several things; pride is one of them.

> The fear of the LORD is to hate evil: pride, and arrogancy, and the evil way, and the froward mouth, do I hate (Proverbs 8:13).

God hates the look of I. Who would want to participate in an act that separates us from the love of God? Our great God is the definition of humility; this is why we have the life we do today. If God were conceited or egotistic, He wouldn't have sacrificed what He did to save us.

As a child, I learned the story of Nebuchadnezzar, the king who was made to live and eat with the beasts of the field and the wild animals because of his pride. Daniel 5:21 describes how he was "Given grass to eat like cattle, and his body was drenched with the dew of heaven." He remained in that state until he reverenced God as the ruler of all humanity. Pride is no match for God. God desires that we walk in humility and obtain grace when we do so.

Take a look at the James 4:6, "God is opposed to the proud, but gives grace to the humble." God gives grace and favor; with that comes provision. I am thankful for God's grace that I do not deserve. God loves us so much that He encourages us through His Word to humble ourselves. Humility knows no ego and is a beautiful attribute. Sometimes it is misunderstood and many think the humble devalue their abilities and self-worth. Contrary to this perception, humility is simply allowing God to be first in all things and restricting room for the enemy to shine.

Pride is a heart problem – an attribute of the enemy. Pride will take you so far just to drop you off. Don't allow it to take root. Pluck it out, uproot it quickly. Stay on your knees before God. Beware. Pride is the greatest of sins, for it is directly against submission to God. Pride is disobedient. It shows up as haughtiness, selfishness, judgment, and hostility resulting in destroyed relationships. But humility is the remedy to pride. The enemy uses pride to keep us from opening our hearts to freedom in Jesus Christ. We must let go of our views and opinions. They do not have the final authority. I'm sure, like me, you've met people who held on to their points of view and refused to admit they were erroneous. Pride.

Pride will take you so far just to drop you off.

Words of reconciliation and forgiveness create beauty. The more we fall in love with Jesus, the deeper our hearts will fall for Christ and His doctrines. His Word. We must be open to love others the way Christ loves us and open enough to receive God's love from others. I want to encourage you to hold fast to this scripture:

> For though we walk in the flesh, we do not war after the flesh: for the weapons of our warfare are not carnal, but mighty through God to the pulling down of strong holds (2 Corinthians 10:3-4).

Commit to the fight. Commit to decreasing in pride every day and in every realm of your life. It never wins. Remember to consider the I.

Words of Life

Father, I completely surrender my heart to You. I ask You to search me as David did in Psalm 139:23-24, "Search me, O God, and know my heart: try me, and know my thoughts and see if there be any wicked way in me, and lead me in the way everlasting." Father, I release every concern and prideful thought to You, so I am not hindered from growing in You. I thank You that the spirit of pride does not have a root in me. I am a shining light to all, and I walk in love and humility. I surrender my will to Yours and I am enriched by Your Word.

The Challenge

Think on 1 Peter 3:4: "Rather, it should be that of your inner self, the unfading beauty of a gentle and quiet spirit, which is of great worth in God's sight." When people see you, do they see pride? Do they see the unfading beauty of a gentle spirit?

Has pride hindered your walk with God? How has this impacted your life?

PROVERB SIXTEEN

MY KINGDOM MAN

Desiring that missing piece, that special one to complement, guide, and protect. Desiring him. The one charged with the care of my heart. I longed for him. That one. One to share my desires and dreams with. One to whom I disclose my innermost secrets. One who would pray ungodliness away and declare love to stay. My safe haven, my teacher, the one God designed to help me with my flaws and catapult me into my destiny. Together, we are ministry.

The Message

My husband and I have twenty-six years together and a lifetime to go. I asked God for an amazing, God-fearing husband and to be married forever when I said, "I do." I vowed to commit my all. I was living with my parents when I got married. My wedding night was the first night I ventured out of their home on my own. As a young girl, I often prayed for someone to love me like Christ loved the church. I needed a man to take good care of my heart. A man who would love me more than he loved himself. Sound bold? Yes, it was! But that was my desire. I already knew how it felt to be heartbroken, and by no means did I want to feel that way again. I wanted godly love. It was pretty farfetched for a small town, simple girl like me, but I knew it was possible. This was my prayer. I knew I was a child of God, and He would grant my heart's desire.

God gave me that love. Now, honestly, those 26 years of marriage weren't all tidy and perfect (especially that first couple of years), but we learned together. We grew together, made honest mistakes together, and prayed through it all. Our time together taught me something about myself. I was that spoiled li'l lady who had to have it her way. Yep, that was me! I learned how to wait and not respond out of emotion – even though I was right at times – well, most times. I asked God to help me select my words so that my husband could hear my heart and not my emotions. They were sometimes scattered and all over the place. I needed someone to lovingly look beyond the sensitivity of my reactions and know my heart's true feelings.

Often, marriages fail because we don't know how to address our mates in ways that honor them and God. We yell, scream, cop an attitude, and roll our eyes. Women, we have to learn how to handle us before we work to address the men we want to see changes in. In the height of my honeymoon, I quickly learned Proverbs 25:24, "Better to live on a corner of the roof than share a house with a quarrelsome wife." That one hit right at home. Men can't handle our mouths. We always have quick comebacks. Like clockwork, it always comes out just perfectly for the discussion we're in. Our timing is impeccable. We are strong and sharp with our tongues. You know exactly what I'm talking about.

When I was newly married, I would become upset at times. I was quick to speak my mind. No wisdom. If I thought it, I'd say it, and I'd holler doing it. One day, my husband grabbed the car keys. I asked where he was going, and he replied, "Anywhere but here. I can't take it." He asked me, "Do you hear yourself?" The truth is, I wasn't listening to him, and I wasn't listening to myself. Beginning that day, I asked the Lord to help me bridle my tongue. It was becoming destructive, and dissension was winning the battle. I knew I had to do something to settle the score.

I was embarrassed that I allowed my mind the power to frame the words I spoke.

Women, we must learn to close our mouths – and listen! Marriage quickly taught me that my husband did not have to agree with everything I said. I didn't have to agree with his thoughts either. My battle was feeling he always had to agree with my feelings. I later learned that as my husband, he was charged with respecting my feelings, and he did that beautifully. When I learned this very important nugget of wisdom, my marriage sweetened. We fell into a whole new level of love that rested in our love and respect for each other.

Every woman desires a man who wishes to help her get to the next level. There is nothing better than a kingdom man who sees your worth, even when you're at your worse. He helps you achieve when you feel you can't, and he presses you to work harder when you want to quit, simply because he believes in you. Despite the obstacles, he carries you while you carry your load. He's your cheerleader, your supporter, your friend.

In the broken stages of my life, my husband pulled me up and out of a victim mentality. Back in the day, I found it quite easy to settle there. It was a comfortable place for me, and I'd set up camp in a heartbeat.

My husband spoke life to me during this time. He encouraged me to resist and refuse to be a defeated statistic of the enemy. Often, He reminded me that I was better than the enemy's schemes. In my weakness, he handled me with care and kindness realizing my fragile state and declaring my queenliness. Yep, you heard right. Even at my lowest, he still treated me and responded to me as his queen.

My mindset began to change. I would not be taken hostage by my emotions or the pain of my past. I chose to become a hostage to his love and security. He covered me and faithfully shielded me from the enemy by watching my blind side. He rebuked all that was not of God, so I might soar and not surrender to past problems or hurts. He decreed no setbacks for me. Why? Because the Word of God was his blueprint for me. On the days he couldn't figure me out, his focus settled on that blueprint and what God called me to be. Through prayer, he called forth my victorious future.

> *He covered me and faithfully shielded me from the enemy by watching my blind side.*

A kingdom man understands the importance of standing up and being the man God called him to be. A kingdom man is a helper, a protector, a leader. Strong. He's a man who fights for his family and protects their well-being. He makes it happen for that family. He puts God first. His foundation is upright, and he bears good fruit. Blessings are born of him. As God's understudy, he is an attractive challenge for the enemy. The foundation is tested because this is what God allows; nevertheless, it is secured in Jesus. When it comes to his helpmeet, the kingdom man may see her dreams ding because of disappointment or rejection but encourages her to keep fighting. He reassures her that God has plans for her success!

> Let us make man in our image, according to our likeness (Genesis 1:26).

God gave man responsibility, authority, and power. All that is out of order falls in line when men submit to the authority of Jesus, Why? Because Christ is in the equation. For years, many men have been absent, retreating and failing to carry out the responsibilities God ordained for them. The wives of such men are neglected and mistreated, but the kingdom man honors what God loves and that is to love his wife.

Our God is searching for kingdom men who know their positions as it pertains to women. God is looking for men who love genuinely, who view their wives as gifts, not possessions. There is a difference. Think about this. Will the kingdom man come forth and build the wall for the family? Will he secure it so no devil in hell can destroy the home front? According to the book of Ephesians, the kingdom man has certain obligations to his wife as she has to him. It's pretty simple.

God is looking for men who love genuinely, who view their wives as gifts, not possessions.

Wives, submit yourselves unto your own husbands, as unto the Lord. For the husband is the head of the wife, even as Christ is the head of the church: and he is the Savior of the body. Therefore as the church is subject unto Christ, so let the wives be to their own husbands in everything. Husbands, love your wives, even as Christ also loved the church, and gave himself for it; that he might sanctify and cleanse it with the washing of water by the word. That he might present it to himself a glorious church, not having spot, or wrinkle, or any such thing; but that it should be holy and without blemish. So ought men to love their wives as their own bodies. He that loveth his wife loveth himself. For no man ever yet hated his own flesh; but nourisheth and cherisheth it, even as the Lord the church (Ephesians 5:22-29).

We call forth the kingdom man who is honest, strong, committed, courageous, balanced, holy, suitable, and fashioned after God's heart. He is a man who operates under the authority of Jesus Christ, handling that woman in love. Together, yes, together, they are a ministry.

Words of Life

Father, I am thankful for my kingdom man, my promise. My heart is content, and my mind is settled because of his love for me. I am satisfied knowing that he loves me as Christ loves the church. Father, I thank You that we are one of the same mind united in the spirit; therefore, our love is sealed with God's approval. I feel so confident in our future. I thank You that the enemy is defeated, and I have a marriage of longevity. I am a godly example to other women, and I conquer all because of You. I declare that my kingdom man will submit to the Lordship of Jesus Christ. My kingdom man loves me as Your Word has instructed him. I am respected and held in high esteem because of the God in him. He is the head of our home, and the family unit is well provided for, lacking nothing. He prays for us and declares the enemy will not come nigh our dwelling place. With You on our side, together we are an unstoppable force.

The Challenge

What are the obstacles you face in submitting to your husband?

What areas of your life can you change to help your relationship?

What is the one special attribute you pray for in a kingdom man and why?

PROVERB SEVENTEEN
THAT OTHER KIND *of* MAN

We're impressed with the label, but we don't check the content of the package. The heart. We're impressed by the tailor-made suit, the Gucci shoes, the alligator wallet that holds the bills displayed at dinner (a top-notch piece within from the counterfeit collection). The suit? Borrowed. The shoes? Returned. The car – yep, mama wants her wheels back. Women, don't be tricked by the representation the enemy sends. Instead, wait on the one God sends. Spare yourself pain, loss, and most importantly, precious time. Verify the contents of the package, not just the shine.

The Message

How do you work through the process? You know what I'm talking about. The process of the relationship turning cold. How is it that you were once so close, and you believed he was your best friend? When you had nothing, you had each other, but now, you're stuck in the daydreams of what was. Listen. It was all a lie from the beginning. These days, you walk alone while people watch your every step. You spent years waiting for this man who made the sacred promise to be your husband, your covering – yes, him. He's gone. It will no longer be; it's over. He's with her now.

Sadly, you ignored the warnings of the mothers. I've been there. I can recall the times I heard, "Daughter, he's not the one God has for you." Have you heard that too? But you failed to take heed of the wisdom because you were caught up in the man. He said all the right things. He had all the good moves. He was slick and yes, he was sexy. The whispers in your ear set you on fire but you failed to check your heart. His heart was wicked, but you trusted it because he made you feel good. You refused to pray for him because he repeatedly told you he loved you. That was enough. He said all the sweet words you longed to hear. But those words were deceptive, cunningly put together just to lure you into his world of mischief. It was a complete, well-orchestrated design of the enemy to keep you from being blessed with the kingdom man God made for you.

Many single women have spent too much time with the wrong man. Honestly, you know he's not the one. You sense it deep in your soul. But after all the years you've invested in his world – and the world you dreamed of with him – you can't let the relationship go. You keep hoping that your dream will come true, and he does just enough to keep you hanging on. Needless to say, holding on is a trick to detour you from receiving God's best.

Sure, letting go is hard. The challenge in overcoming is the shame and embarrassment. Next, regret and feelings of loneliness surface. You'd rather settle for that other kind of man than to be alone. For this reason, many of us remain stuck in relationships that are physically, verbally, and emotionally abusive. I know it's hard to work through the painful process and believe you'll love again, or better yet, know someone will love you. I know it's tough, but you have to let him go. God has a greater plan.

How many can admit to being caught up in the outer shell? The money was good, but it was fast money. The cash isn't worth the heartache if he can't surrender his heart to you. The flip side is he hasn't the stability to keep you winning. Winning is something you deserve! There is nothing like a man who can't provide for you. The church mothers warned you. Don't let this information go over your head. If he says he hasn't worked in five years, believe him. Listen, pay attention, take note, and watch to see if he will produce. Trust your heart. Trust your instincts. If you are stuck in a dead-end relationship, by God's grace, you will be free.

Sisters, do you remember the red flags? There may have been many. I understand how our emotions run everywhere. You think he will change one day. He won't change. He won't. Remember, God already told you he is not the one. Don't get married and expect him to change. It will only get worse. We've all been in love, but love doesn't pay the bills. You deserve better. You do. Wait on God for your blessing. My girlfriend's powerful saying is, "Don't be stuck on stupid till when good comes, you miss it." Love yourself. You are better than a fairy tale wrapped up in a lie. You are better than seconds and better than thirds.

The progression of any prosperous relationship starts by acknowledging God first. God is your best point of reference. It's a beautiful feeling to desire to be that special woman in a man's life, but he has to be the right man God has for you. That's when it's special. The ungodly man expects a woman to let him continue to be self-absorbed. I want to encourage you to get absorbed in God and trust Him to give you His very best! Be watchful who you tie your soul to. It is costly! Ungodly intimate soul ties must be broken by the power of the Holy Ghost in order to move on. Don't open yourself to demonic activity. Remember that old saying, "If you lie down with dogs, you get up with fleas."[1] So it is in the spirit realm. Watch your connections closely.

> *The progression of any prosperous relationship starts by acknowledging God first.*

Sex. It's a beautiful thing God's way. Good sex gets old when you're constantly second. Why remain second when you can be first? Ladies, don't settle for a counterfeit blessing. Wait for the gift God tailor-made for you. There is power, satisfaction, peace, and happiness in your waiting – and after! If you fail to wait, the fall is painful. Why be in pain? Why suffer when you don't have to? I get it; a piece of a man is better than going without one. Oh, but the joy of connecting with the right one! One of the hardest things to do is wait. I know; I've been there. Sometimes it's difficult while waiting to find a meaningful purpose to center your life around. I encourage you to make God your center while you wait. In your season of waiting, God will invest in you, building you up to be the woman you desire to be. In your waiting, God can teach you to love yourself over loving the other kind of man. Don't you think you deserve

1   https://thecornfedpastor.wordpress.com/2013/02/15/if-you-lie-down-with-dogs-you-get-up-with-fleas/

a good thing, a better thing? Yes, you do! We all do. God can fill the void you may be feeling – the remnants of past relationships. You are worth it! You are worth everything God has promised you. Wait on God; trust Him to bless you with the man you deserve. A kingdom man!

Words of Life

Father, I thank You that I have Your patience right now to WAIT! You know what is best for my life. When waiting gets heavy and lonely, I will pray earnestly to stay focused on having the best. I thank You, Lord, that You minister to me through Your Word daily, and I am stronger than my thoughts and my flesh. I declare and decree that I will not settle for anything less than what You have for me. While I wait, I will serve You, Lord, with my whole heart. I will take the time to acknowledge You first. I reference You as my King, and I submit to You with my whole heart. Thank You, Lord, for Your love and grace towards me. By faith, I am now victorious in areas of weaknesses. I place my hope and confidence in You.

The Challenge

Take the time to seek the Lord for direction by going on a seven-day consecration. Seek the Lord to break soul ties of the past by acknowledging God in your life. During those seven days, write down what you earnestly need God to do in your life.

Pray and meditate on the Word. Empty yourself before God and thank Him in advance for strength to wait for your kingdom man.

SAFE, SECURE
and
SETTLED

I was ecstatic from the first day I heard your heartbeat. I love you with a love that cannot be described. You were made for me, my darling child. Heaven sent me a special gift that would make me proud and one day grow to call me blessed. I am to be a good steward and handle you with care. God blessed me to be a parent – the best parent, mother, for you. I pray for you all the time, often more than I pray for myself. This world won't have you; it dare not try, for you are a righteous seed, a royal seed. You are mine.

The Message

Not too long ago, the Holy Spirit spoke to me. His words were clear as crystal, "You are to be a good steward of your children." I took those words close to my heart and obeyed the voice of the Holy Spirit with conviction. We are blessed with children to look after, cherish, and protect. Love them as you love yourself. Lead them as if their destinies depend on it, for they do. Women, love your children as you love that man. God is watching; therefore, we must carry out the instructions our Father has given us. Hold that child in high esteem; your reward will be great.

> Lo, children are a heritage of the Lord: and the fruit
> of the womb is his reward (Psalm 127:3).

Parents, praise God for your reward. Praise Him for favor. Foster your heritage. I challenge you to invest in your heritage as God has invested in you. It's an honor and privilege to keep our children dear in our deeds and words.

God favored you with a seed that would grow to become brilliant and talented with an overflow of treasure, wealth, and wisdom. Why would you not value what God has blessed you with? Why would you not take the time to invest in your children's character? Why wouldn't you equip them with the tools needed to win and thrive in life? Parents, our children need us to be sounding boards and a constant source of encouragement; our hands are to help and our voices to give aid. We are their intercessors, standing in the gap, interrupting the fiery darts of the enemy with prayer. Prayer transcends to the spirit realm and appears before the court of heaven. Jesus intercepts those prayers and communicates them to the Father who watches over our children. Some children are challenges and the enemy casually makes it seem as if they will never change or progress. Nevertheless, never give up on your seed. Ever.

I will forever remember a valuable conversation I had with Lady Kimberly Watkin. With tears in her eyes, she reflected, "What do you do when God instructs you to be quiet and pray when your seed is in trouble?" With concern and compassion, she responded to her question.

There is nothing more painful than seeing your children go through pain, and you can't help them. She was unquestionably confident that God encourages us, as parents, to stand in faith and trust in His deliverance. Sometimes, God allows our children to go through, so the results are testimonies of God's grace and power. He builds our children in preparation for what they will need later. Our position is on our knees. We must have a vigilant stance in prayer that every assignment of the enemy is canceled! Every single one. Don't stop praying. Don't stop standing in faith for a miracle. Anticipate a victory no matter what it looks like. Stand on the Word of God for the deliverance of our children! When we look through the eternal lens of God, we discover that He sees the bigger picture.

Our children are the future church and nation. The world can't have them. We declare that our wonder-working God touches their hearts to help them understand they cannot make it without Him. We must pray that they are God-conscious and reverence God as their Creator. Like you, I am concerned. We live in a day when parents are not investing in their rewards. I can recall the many times my daughters needed something financially and my husband and I were not in a position to provide as we would have liked, but we gave them our last. As long as we had food in our refrigerator and gas in our vehicles, we gave them our last to provide what they needed. We promised our children we would not be crutches for them. Rather, we would support them as long as they worked hard to be successful in life. We took time to teach them the value of having good credit and keeping a good name.

We must pray that they are God-conscious and reverence God as their Creator.

> A good name is rather to be chosen than great riches, and
> loving favor rather than silver and gold (Proverbs 22:1).

They were our responsibility. Therefore, we taught them to respect themselves and not allow the enemy to make them look bad. I would always tell my daughters before they left home for outings, "Don't let your name beat you back home. Watch your character!" They are adults now but the lesson still applies. Eighteen years old doesn't necessarily make someone grown; it's simply a new chapter of learning and living.

Parents, do you remember 18 when you were unwise in your decisions, fragile at facing challenges, and intimidated by life and all it had to offer? Do you remember the times you made costly mistakes? We've all been there. These days are unlike my young adulthood. The world has changed drastically becoming wicked and cold. In fact, it's colder than it ever was. We must help our children be wise and discerning. Teach them how to watch for the enemy. Teach them how to rebuke the devil because there are consequences should they decide to give in. I'm not talking about preaching to them but taking time to teach them the way of the Lord. Parents, stay on your watch. Don't leave your post. Stay right there until that child is ready to fly out of the nest. It's your duty and your obligation!

At times, parenting can mean taking on the role of a counselor and being concerned about every aspect of the child's growth and development. As a counselor, stand firm while directing each step and advising as Christ would. The development of our children goes far beyond infancy. It's caring in the midnight hour. It comes with apprehension about where your children are and who their friends are. It comes with big concerns for your children and their overall well-being.

I will never forget a sermon I heard preached by Pastor Roland Banks. He titled it, "You Show Me Your Friends, and I Will Show You Your Future." Teach your children early what friends look like from God's perspective. Parents, wake up! Check their phones. Check who's on their social media. Where are your children at night? Do they reside in your house? Search their bedrooms. Respect and love are essential in your house. In our home, the lesson was, "Yes, you're grown, but you still live here so you will attend church." Staying home was not an option.

I learned to pray constantly for understanding, patience, and wisdom to know my daughters' characters and tendencies. Most importantly, I learned how to treat my daughters with respect, as young ladies. I learned not to abuse them with my words just because I was Mama. In fact, the opposite applies. Because I am their mom, they deserve my respect. I didn't beat them up with attitudes, which, in my opinion, cause wedges in relationships. I didn't want my daughters to be intimidated or frustrated in our relationship. I didn't act contrary to God's Word. My stance as a mother was to be an example of holiness, guiding in love, not ruling with criticism. Many women today say they are Christians. However, this is the true question you should answer: are you holy? Are you set apart from worldly behavior?

Our children are watching us. As much as we think they are distracted by the lights and glam of the world, they are soaking in everything we do and say. We dare not want our lifestyles or words to backfire. "Don't fight them so hard that they become the very thing we prayed they'd never be." Well said by Nathalie, my friend and co-worker. This spoke volumes to me. In most cases, our children are reflections of who we are. Therefore, we must mirror the right spirit for them. Sisters, instill in them a desire – a need – to pray and love the Lord above all things. Above all, teach your children to grow in love with God and to grow in obedience to the Lord.

In today's society, our young men are in need of help. Most are hurting due to the absence of their father or father-figure; mothers shouldn't raise them alone. Our prison cells are full. Our young men need godly mentors. They need true men to teach them not to be included in the statistics we hear too often. They need a reliable resource. A consistent presence. Too many of our young men are dropped. Dropped as in – Dad left and now he's filled with anger due to abandonment and loss. We see this too often as our young men demonstrate the pain they feel by way of violence.

Mothers, pray for your sons and let their fathers be the fathers they need.

Fathers, our sons need you. Yes, they need your financial support, but that is not sufficient – not now, not ever. Most importantly, they need your genuineness, your constant love, and the check-in phone calls. They long for you to ask about their day, how they're doing in school, and about their friends and acquaintances. They need you to show concern. They need you to show up, not just physically, but mentally, emotionally, and financially. They need you, all of you, for all of them. Your seed. Take care of it as you care for yourself. Please, be more than a donor. Be more! Be reminded of this scripture:

> But if any provide not for his own, and especially for
> those of his own house, he hath denied the faith, and
> is worse than an infidel (1 Timothy 5:8).

The Word. Period. Should you be a stepfather or stepmother, remember, you know the Word of God. Be fair. Maybe the children are not yours biologically but you must still love them with the love of the Lord. It's not the child's fault that Mom or Dad remarried. It's not the child's fault that Mom and Dad didn't make it together. Remember, children are rewards from the Lord. We have a responsibility to them.

Fathers, love your daughters. Teach them before the men in the world show them a different type of love, an abusive love, a condescending love. I asked a friend, Raquel, who lost her father at a young age, to describe how he made her feel. Her response was simple but powerful. "My father's love for me was so pure. It was like he could see clearly through my soul and knew what he wanted me to become. He knew what I was made of, and what I was up against in this life. God gave me to him, and he died taking care of his responsibilities." His responsibilities. Yes, his responsibilities. Her response reminded me of my husband and the impact he has on the lives of our daughters. I recall my husband taking our daughters out on their very first dates. He demonstrated to them how they should be treated and what to expect from a godly man. They were taught to never accept being last but always first – next to God. Never settle. Never compromise. Never waiver in who they are as young women of God.

Fathers, teach your daughters early so they will grow to be wise and listen to the voice of their heavenly Father when making decisions. Many young women today have homeless mentalities. Their emotions have no place to rest. They've been abused or mistreated as children so much that they are depressed – without the mental stability to win in life. A mentally homeless state causes one to look vigilantly to another person for validation. Therefore, these women remain trapped within themselves and cannot live out the beauty God's freedom gives.

Mothers, teach your daughters how to be fearless and beautiful; they are righteous seeds. Declare they will grow to be brilliant and have the strength to take on life's trials. Pray for their triumphs and successes. Speak life into their lives so they will not succumb to the opinions of others but adhere to the truth of the Word. Our daughters find safety in a mother's love – simply in our presence at times. Mothers, when you buy yourself a dress, buy your daughter one too. When you get your hair done, make an appointment for your daughter too. Teach them how to put on perfume and deodorant and the importance of being cognizant of their appearance and personal hygiene. It's real, and you know it! Women of today, we are obligated to impart words of wisdom, skill sets, and knowledge into the lives of the young women of tomorrow. It is our duty as mothers and women.

My dear friend Marie was a single mother who worked full time. I witnessed her raise a son and two young ladies who grew up to be intelligent and successful. She was a single mom for years, and she promised herself she would not marry until they graduated high school. She desired to give them her undivided attention. She did not allow men in and out of her home. She protected them and refused to allow them to see any streaks in the mirror of what could very well be their future. She demonstrated the importance of giving attention to the people in life who mattered. She invested in her seeds as treasures from the Lord.

Our children are rewards. Mothers and fathers, spend quality time with your great rewards from God. I can't help but reflect on conversations I've had with mothers who have had to combat in prayer for their sons declaring their success.

Renee Winston's son, Easop, is attending Washington State University on a full athletic scholarship. His promotion didn't come easy due to dynamics in the home. His classes became challenging, and he went through a season of sadness knowing he could do better. He was consumed with the pressures of life as a new college student. The faithful and enduring prayers of his mother latched on to his spirit and without fail, he recovered all. Not some. All. I remember his mother praying and declaring war that the enemy would not steal the dream her son desired.

The power of a praying mother will go into the enemy's camp and take back all he has stolen! Believe it! Her declaration to her son, Easop, was, "Only God can do it," and our great God did! God recompensed him for all he had lost.

BJ is a quiet, smart, and profoundly talented basketball player; however, he had his challenges while in junior college. His mother, Regina, faithfully visited him to ensure that he was doing well. Although BJ was an adult (student-athlete) in college, he was her responsibility. She felt obligated to ensure he had the best. That's what a mother does. She would not let him fail. She kept her hands in his business (lol). At times, it appears the enemy has a plan, but God has a greater plan. BJ is doing outstandingly well as a senior at Bellevue University. He has had a successful basketball career receiving several awards and breaking records. Never give up on your seed; your investment is worth it. You will receive an invaluable return.

My dear friend, Deanna, has a son, Clinton, who is currently a student at Morehouse College. In his sophomore year of high school, his grades began to drop. It's never easy for students when peers are bullying them. I remember his mother telling me, "Not on my watch. He will not be a statistic. He will graduate high school, and he will do great in life." Just as she shared those words with me, she spoke them over her son's life. She withdrew Clinton from St. John Bosco High School and enrolled him in an all-boys military academy to equip him with the discipline and help needed to tap into his God-given potential. Clinton returned to St. John Bosco High and graduated with honors. A dedicated mother – his dedicated mother – focused on her son's academic success. She did not lose sight of his promising future. Although the steps to create change were uncomfortable and challenging, Clinton's mother knew the reward would be greater.

I had a conversation with a mother, Deborah, whose son was incarcerated in a California correctional institution for five years. While visiting her son, she was disturbed when he told her he was made to take showers in cold water. When she returned home from her visit, she vicariously lived the life of her son by taking a cold shower to see what it felt like. With deep distress for him, she told me, "It felt like needles piercing my skin." She tried to stay in the shower as long as she could, but jumped out quickly, fell on her knees, and cried.

Later that same day, after she pulled herself together, determined, she called a friend who worked at a prison and asked for guidance on how to help her son. This friend told her who to contact in order of rank. She learned the order of rankings as a sergeant, lieutenant, captain, chief deputy warden, and finally, the warden. The Lord put it in Deborah's spirit to call the captain. With favor, she was able to speak to the captain about her son's predicament and demanded to know why. She boldly, but respectfully asked the captain, "Have you ever taken a cold shower yourself?" He responded, "Yes." She then asked him how it felt. There was a long pause on the line. She told him if he did not turn on the hot water, she would call every local media outlet and also retain a lawyer for the inhumane treatment her son endured.

Five days later, Deborah received a call from her son. He explained to her that he was lying on his bed in his cell when he heard an announcement over the loudspeaker, "V49934, get dressed." Four officers came to his cell and told him to put on his prison suit. He was escorted to see the captain. The captain asked him if he told anyone he was not able to take warm showers, then he asked who Deborah Bradford was. V49934 responded, "She's my mama." The captain then told him he was turning the hot water on, and he could call his mother to let her know. V49934 returned to his cell, telling the other inmates the hot water was on because his mama called the captain. A mother's love is powerful. Unconditional!

Mothers, we must allow our sons and daughters to see the fight in us for them. The power of the Holy Ghost spoke through this mother and touched the captain's heart to turn the hot water on. V49934 – Charles Williams – is graduating from college at 41 years old in the spring of 2018 – by faith! Mothers, when it comes down to your children, do not take "No" for an answer. Command the hands of the enemy to be blocked, stopped, and held back. What would a mother not do for her son? A mother will sacrifice for the well-being of her children. Seeing them succeed is the best feeling in the world.

The love and commitment devoted to your children unquestionably make a difference in their promising futures. Your investment will have a great return. Your seed and inheritance are rewards from the Lord. I challenge you, parents – mothers and fathers – to accept responsibility for the overall growth of your children. Take pride in guiding them in life so they can be victorious at each task they set out to accomplish. Teach them that in life, there will be challenges, but with the help of the Lord, they will succeed no matter the test. We declare that in Christ they are safe, secured, and settled!

Words of Life

Father, I thank You that my seed is blessed, and I cherish the reward You have given me. I give my children back to You. I value the amazing love You have placed in their hearts for Your Word. They will grow to be obedient, holding fast to Your principles. Thank You that our children are successful, lacking nothing, and every need is provided. The blood of Jesus covers them. By faith, they will be contributing citizens in their communities and worldwide because they represent everything You are. Our children will be brilliant and courageous with Your help. They will do great exploits on the earth for Your glory.

The Challenge

What challenges have you faced in raising your children?

How have you used such challenges to positively impact their lives?

YOU SEE MY FLAWS, *but* GOD SEES DIFFERENTLY

Who said we can't wear red? Why can't the saints be color-blind like God seeing the heart rather than the physical? The emphasis, the red nails, the red shoes, and the fitted dress, was it a sin? And the bright colored lipstick! Sweet-spirited purity at its finest. Brand new in Christ, but she wore red. Did we forget that the blood of Jesus was red? He paid it all for our sins.

The Message

Praise and worship are explosive. But because the praise and worship leader is wearing a fitted red dress, many are not even conscious of the worship experience. Their minds are not drawn to a heart that creates an atmosphere of worship but distracted by inappropriate attire, in their opinion. God is bigger than color and clothing. However, we get so caught up in our thoughts and how we feel. I used the example of red and the fitted dress to describe how we often spend unnecessary mental energy on things that are irrelevant to God.

Yes, there are pre-existing standards of modesty to uphold. However, many who have hearts to "police" attire would rather spotlight the detail of someone's appearance, instead of promoting God's love. We are living in a time when we must extend Jesus by demonstrating love to gain souls, not lose them. Our mission is to win souls, not judge them. Does a person's style or color of dress determine his/her level in the Lord? No, it doesn't. There are so many people, more than ever before, searching for truth and answers to some hard questions. These people won't find what they are looking for if there isn't an authentic demonstration of God's love. Christians must prepare themselves to receive those who are unchurched and unconventional despite their tattoos, body piercings, and bright hair color. We see flaws, but God sees differently.

He sees the heart. He's ultimately concerned about the soul.

People from all walks of life are searching to fill inner voids, which can only be filled by Jesus. When church congregations are full of what we are not used to, we must embrace these differences with love, not judgment. The revelation of the Word and God-encounters bring about conversion that starts first in the minds and hearts – the two areas we cannot see naturally. These people, the ones whose appearances don't blend with tradition, are still God's creation. Reshaping the heart and mind is God's handiwork and responsibility. Outer change becomes evident with time when we allow God to perfect His plan and purpose for His people. Our position should be to partner with Him by fulfilling the command to love as He does.

I'm sure you have heard the old saying, "You can't skin a fish before you catch it." It is our Christian duty to display love. We must function from a place that acknowledges and understands that God shows us love by covering us in our imperfections. Love teaches us that to walk in the blessings of God, we have to be brave enough to say, "Lord, show me what is in my heart. Clarify the things I do not understand, so I don't interfere with your ultimate plan. Convict me where I am missing the mark. Destroy any mindset or deep-seated belief that does not align with your Word. Help me to see the truth about my life. Expose me, God, to myself, so I can make changes that last." Have a sincere conversation with the Lord, and He will speak to your soul with love.

Love does not initially say, "Take that dress off; it's too tight. Wipe that lipstick off; it's too red," but love says, "Let's have a chat. Let's have a heart-to-heart." Love asks a question, "What can I help you with?" God is concerned about our inner-beings, our hearts. God desires that we pour our hearts out to Him sincerely. I admire David's genuine heartfelt prayer to God.

> Have mercy upon me, O God, according to thy lovingkindness: according unto the multitude of thy tender mercies blot out my transgressions. Wash me thoroughly from mine iniquity, and cleanse me from my sin. For I acknowledge my transgressions: and my sin is ever before me. Against thee, thee only, have I sinned, and done this evil in thy sight: that thou mightest be justified when thou speakest, and be clear when thou judgest. Behold, I was shapen in iniquity; and in sin did my mother conceive me. Behold, thou

desirest truth in the inward parts: and in the hidden part thou shalt make me to know wisdom. Purge me with hyssop, and I shall be clean: wash me, and I shall be whiter than snow. Make me to hear joy and gladness; that the bones which thou hast broken may rejoice. Hide thy face from my sins, and blot out all mine iniquities. Create in me a clean heart, O God; and renew a right spirit within me (Psalm 51:10).

David came to God sincerely. What I love about this Psalm is that David speaks of taking responsibility for his actions. David didn't try to trick God as if God didn't already know. God knew David's heart and its inner workings. We must teach newcomers that God knows what we have done, but He wants us to build our relationship with Him so that we can be open about what we have done. We must provide practical strategies showing them how to unveil themselves before God to grow, rather than judge them and add more pain and confusion. It seems as though many churchgoers have forgotten they have not always lived sin-free lives, and they too were recipients of God's grace. The grace of God, which was shown to you, ought to be the same mercy and compassion given to newcomers in the kingdom.

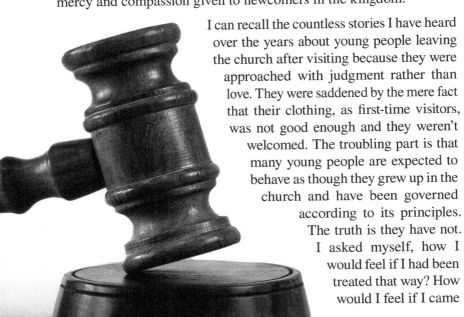

I can recall the countless stories I have heard over the years about young people leaving the church after visiting because they were approached with judgment rather than love. They were saddened by the mere fact that their clothing, as first-time visitors, was not good enough and they weren't welcomed. The troubling part is that many young people are expected to behave as though they grew up in the church and have been governed according to its principles. The truth is they have not. I asked myself, how I would feel if I had been treated that way? How would I feel if I came looking for something unique and hoping for a change to occur in my life but was unable to feel the presence of God? How would I handle the judgmental stares, the blatant glares, the whispers, and the cold and overt mistreatment just because I didn't look a certain way?

Sadly, many have left churches and the idea of being connected to the church as a path to God for unanswered questions and inner healing. To this day, many refuse to return due to the painful experience of rejection. God doesn't approve of this behavior because He is love. He loves us so much that He looks beyond our shortcomings and still deems us worthy of love, grace and mercy. Mature saints cannot forget how God accepted and was patient with us. God's heart toward His children is priceless, and we must adopt the same posture. Matthew cautions us:

> If anyone causes one of these little ones–those who believe in me–to stumble, it would be better for them to have a large millstone hung around their neck and to be drowned in the depths of the sea (Matthew 18:6 NIV).

You see my flaws, but God sees me differently. Although different in my choice of style and attire, don't hurt, mishandle, or judge me. We cannot afford to be the reason someone runs before we can help them. I cannot even imagine someone hurting my children. The scripture is clear about how God feels when someone disappoints His children. Who are the little ones Matthew 18:6 speaks of? I see the little ones as those who were not fortunate enough to have been in church for years. I see the little ones desiring to fit in but not really knowing how to. I see the little ones desiring to dress better but may not have the means to. They're barely making it on what they have. The little ones who scarcely come to church arriving at the house of God in broken pieces. They come expecting a blessing but upon arrival, feel condemned.

I used the color red as a symbol of the blood of Jesus. Jesus shed His blood on Calvary for you and me, so we might have a chance to live victoriously and be free. Jesus covered the penalty for our mistakes and those of every human being once and for all. As He hung on the cross for our hang-ups, let us not forget the cost of God's provision for a better life. We see flaws, but God sees differently.

Words of Life

Father God, I am delivered from a judgmental spirit because I choose to see what You see. I love who You love, and I hear what You hear. I thank You for consuming me with Your compassionate Spirit, which allows me to look beyond faults and see needs. I thank You that Your Word has taught me to love and embrace others. All souls are Yours, Lord. We all belong to You, and You love all Your children the same. You see all of our flaws, and we thank You for mercy and forgiveness nevertheless. Your love is priceless, and we thank You for Your transforming power.

The Challenge

How can you help those who have been wounded because they did not feel good enough?

How can you make them understand that God loves them, and He sees them differently?

I AM
GREATER
than
FEAR

We can overcome, conquer, and defeat it. If given the opportunity, it can paralyze one's emotions. It is famous for causing anxiety, leaving an individual feeling breathless. It is a counterfeit of my faith and the best friend to the enemy. It's not of God and not a friend, but one invites it in to take counsel. It's a paranoia that presents a threat due to the unknown. It. Is. Fear.

The Message

We get complacent and accept what the enemy feeds us. We let the enemy remain in our lives and bring up things from the past which cause us to develop the fear of moving forward. We embrace our fears and allow the enemy to inhabit the things that don't belong to him: our freedom and our peace. Fear can be a powerful force. Fear targets your mind and emotions and attempts to consume you completely. These emotions will keep you in a holding pattern. They will cripple, paralyze, and send you into a paranoid panic attack. The things we should embrace, we cut off, and what we should cut off, we embrace. Your mind doesn't belong to the devil. 2 Timothy 1:7 empowers us, "For God hath not given us the spirit of fear; but of power, and of love, and of a sound mind." No matter what it looks like, be confident that you have a sound mind, and fear will not win over God. We must cut off the thoughts of the enemy and embrace God's Word, which is total freedom. The Word sets us free and equips us to realize we are greater than fear.

> Ye are of God, little children, and have overcome them: because greater is he that is in you, than he that is in the world (1 John 4:4).

Fear crowds the spirits of many and causes them to stop living. Have you ever gone through something so distressing in your life that it caused you to stop doing the very thing you loved the most? Maybe it was the death of a mate that induced the fear of loving someone again. Fear of losing someone again is unimaginable. However, it is important to realize that the enemy intends to keep us captive to fear, but God wants us delivered and made whole.

God does not desire that we come to church to just shout emotionally on top of the Word. He wants us to receive it. It is not God's desire that we hear the Word and wrap a bandage around our wounds. He desires that we are healed completely. Many things in this life intimidate us, and often, our chief enemy is in the midst of them. In our thoughts, hearts, and minds, we are absorbed by fear. There is a constant struggle to be free but never a complete win.

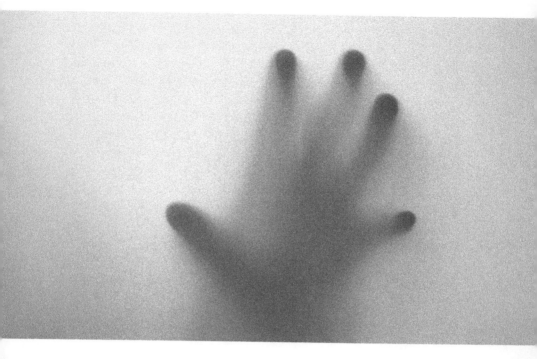

How can we stop the pattern of destructive thinking? How can you break the strongholds of fear? By living on the authority of the Word – by standing strong and declaring that the spirit of fear is destroyed. The Word is our oasis in the wilderness of fear. It is the Word of God that brings us out of situations and takes us through the course of life.

Life, for some, has not been easy. Some of the things you experienced were not your fault, but it happened. Because it happened, allow it to make you. Don't let it break you. Satan has the power to do things according to the flesh because he is the prince of the air. He does not have authority over the spiritual realm. As believers of Christ, we must walk in the Spirit. When you walk in the Spirit of God, you have admittance to possess the divine. The Word proclaims:

> For the weapon of our warfare are not carnal but mighty through God to the pulling down of strong holds (2 Corinthians 10:4).

Our weapons are not of the flesh. They are in the spiritual realm. We have
victory over this tormenting emotion, fear. Satan has imprisoned God's
people for too long. The Lord of the breakthrough has come to grant
you a personal victory leading you to triumph over fear. Triumph!
Victory! If you desire to achieve that personal victory, you must turn
to a position of faith. Affirm your freedom. Bind fear and every negative
thought that prevents you from being free. Declare all curses against
you insignificant, canceled, and harmless. Don't let fear cause you to
just exist, having prosperity, but no peace, a mind but no dominion
over it. Don't allow fear to steal the Word that has been deposited in
your life. Reject fear and intimidation and choose to walk in authority.
Do not let fear suppress you by causing you to relive your past when
God is trying to move you forward. Our Great God wants us to thrive
in life. In spite of how we feel and what life presents, we must live to
the fullest and walk in God's divine will. By faith, you will have victory
in every area of your life!

> *Bind fear and every negative thought that*
> *prevents you from being free.*

You will be the head and not the tail. Fear is under your feet. You are
greater than fear; God said so. You have to believe it and walk in your
deliverance. When faced with sudden fear, God is your defense. He is
with you every step of the way. You must decree and declare that you
can breathe. You will make it and fear will not control your life.

> So do not fear, for I am with you; do not be dismayed, for
> I am your God. I will strengthen you and help you; I will
> uphold you with my righteous right hand (Isaiah 41:10).

You are greater than fear.

Words of Life

I thank You, Lord, that I walk in the authority of the Word and fear will not continue to hold me in bondage. I am greater than fear, and I am free from the plans of the adversary. The deceptive tricks to make me believe his lies won't work. I see no fear because I see the blood of Jesus. The feeling of fear will not consume my mind and emotions. My Redeemer lives; therefore, I am free.

The Challenge

Pray and ask God to reveal to you what causes you to walk in the spirit of fear.

Write a personal confession that applies to the truth God revealed to you and apply scripture to your confession.

For God has not given us a spirit of fear, but of power and of love and of a sound mind. (2 Timothy 1:7)

PROVERB TWENTY-ONE

NEVER too LATE to BE FREE

You have an innermost desire to be free, but the enemy has a stronghold on your life. There is a demonic spirit that keeps you in a holding pattern. It is a strategic design of the enemy, but Jesus has all power to set you free.

And he was teaching in one of the synagogues on the Sabbath. And, behold, there was a woman, who had a spirit of infirmity eighteen years, and was bowed together, and could in no wise could she lift herself. And when Jesus saw her, he called her to him, and said unto her, Woman, thou art loosed from thine infirmity. And he laid his hands on her: and immediately she was made straight, and glorified God (Luke 13:10-13).

The Message

What a glorious testimony. We don't always share the stories of what we have really been through. Why don't we share? Transparency is powerful, but it takes courage. Strength. It takes someone being delivered to share his/her truth. Someone needs to hear our stories to be set free. We must share our stories of the strongholds that kept us in bondage. We must expose the secret things that once crippled us.

Interestingly, we don't mind sharing what makes us look good. In life, people look at the blessings and successes of an individual. The focus is on the arrival, not the journey. The journey to success and deliverance is in the beginning and the middle. Many cannot imagine the sufferings, lessons, tests, setbacks, highs, lows, and the ugly stuff that had to be endured to reach the destination. We just see the end. We camouflage our pain, hurt, and disappointments dreading that someone may see us differently.

> *We camouflage our pain, hurt, and disappointments dreading that someone may see us differently.*

We don't share the negatives because we are afraid that people will judge us by our life experiences failing to look at who we will become in Christ Jesus. This may not sound like you, but it was unquestionably me. There were seasons in my life where I was stuck waiting for God to answer prayers. At least, this is the picture the enemy painted.

In the beforementioned passage in Luke, the woman depicted could not move forward. Stuck! She saw life from a place of defeat and brokenness for eighteen years. Nevertheless, her life would later be a testimony of God's love and deliverance. She had a spirit of infirmity, a bodiless and invisible force that sucks the body of life, energy, and power. The woman was feeble, lacking physical strength and completely defenseless. This spirit was superior to her body.

Interestingly, the book of Luke does not reveal the specific disease that afflicted her body for eighteen years. Have you ever taken the time to ask God about the very thing that is combating your life and preventing you from moving forward? Like this woman, what was your infirmity? What was your bondage? What door did you open? What caused so much pain that you could not lift yourself for countless years? What generational porthole did you expose yourself to that has dominated your life in one form or another? God gives us a remedy; let's explore the Word to receive freedom from bondage.

> I give you the keys to the kingdom and whatever you bind on earth will be bound in heaven, whatever you loose on earth will be loosed in heaven (Matthew 16:19).

God has given us kingdom authority; we must walk in it. This woman had no spiritual resistance; she had no power to fight. Her spiritual immune system was at an all-time low. A spirit can dominate you. It can drastically shift your atmosphere, leave you in a daze, and eventually alter your life's perception. Sadly, you can entertain this demonic spirit in your thoughts and with the words you release from your mouth. Sure enough, it will hold you captive and produce negative outcomes: depression, lack, oppression, etc.

Spirits can alter your ability to make sound decisions. Many people are oppressed by spirits that don't even belong to them. They are fighting battles that are not theirs. Be careful what you entertain. Demonic forces are real, and if you are not strong in God, you will be overpowered. This infirmity (spirit) had great power over this woman. It caused her to be bent over for eighteen years. It was a stronghold of the enemy keeping her from being free. Was this ever you? Spirits are counterfeits, pretenders, and forms that keep you from really knowing God.

The enemy is a big bully who does not play fair. In our times of rest and contentment, he will buffet us. He fights hard. He fights to kill. He challenges us daily. Nevertheless, we have the power to speak deliverance to the very thing that has us in bondage. While reading the story of this woman, I learned that, for some of us, deliverance does not come easily; it is a process. By fasting, praying, and taking kingdom authority through the Word, we shall overcome. My friend, God has given us power over things that are not of Him. Deliverance and healing are our covenant rights.

According to your faith be it unto you (Matthew 9:29b).

You must command the ungodly spirit in your life to be loosed by faith. This woman could in no wise lift herself. Think about those times when you didn't think you could make it but God intervened on your behalf. It is only because of God's grace you were not consumed by the enemy. It's a great feeling when love sees you. Jesus saw her hurt, rejection, brokenness, and the friends who left her. He saw the man who left her, the one who made all those promises. Jesus saw her unachieved goals, broken dreams, and the lies that were told on her. Jesus saw her, not just on that day, but He saw the eighteen-year journey she had traveled. The eighteen-year journey of pain.

Jesus laid His hands on her and set her free. Healing was released in her life. She was redeemed from the curse of infirmity, and it was love that lifted her. Significantly, she went to church where the presence of God was. Don't stay home. Go to church. Take a step of faith. Leave your comfort zone. Meet God and allow Him to transform your life into wholeness. Friends, no matter the situation, no matter the infirmity, don't give up! Continue to stand in faith knowing that our great God will deliver as His Word promises. God will not leave you crippled. He will not leave you stuck. Declare yourself better through the Word.

> Nay, in all these things we are more than conquerors through him that loved us (Romans 8:37).

Words of Life

God's healing power has delivered me from my past afflictions. Thank You that Your hand of mercy touched me in my brokenness. Father, I walk in freedom knowing You are leading me and guiding me on my path to victory. I trust You to help me stand strong in the midst of adversity. I am stronger and better than yesterday. I'm grateful that Your love has set me free. I declare absolute restoration in my life.

The Challenge

Seek the Lord through prayer and ask God to help you identify what has kept you from moving forward in life. Be honest with yourself.

Ask God to lead you to a scripture that will help you remain free.

To HONOR HER IS *the* GREATEST JOY

She bears our pain and confronts our fears. She sees the best in any situation and always stands near. We are here because she was here first. To always reference and respect the beauty of her presence is an honor. Grace is a branch from her loins, and intelligence is birthed while on her knees. Strength is an attribute of her discipline. Oh, how I love you, Mother.

The Message

I can recall the numerous times when I needed someone to talk to, someone to be there just to listen to me talk. Has this ever been you? Have you ever needed someone to listen to you without being judgmental or biased, only to comfort? I needed someone who would listen when I didn't even make sense. Taking the time to express your heart makes things better. There is nothing like a mother listening to you, and you feeling her concern and love for your problems. A mother will be there when everyone else fails you. She is your support system. She is your guide through the deep, dark tunnel. She supplies the hand that rescues you from the deep hole you have fallen into. She helps you to find your way out to a safe place. When all the props are taken away, she never abandons you. She is your balance when life gets chaotic.

As I continuously reflect, what would I do without a mother? When I couldn't figure life out, she taught me how to live each day one day at a time. She taught me how to take life minute by minute or second by second. Her wisdom was like no other; she just made sense to my confused state. Her prayers reached heaven on my behalf, and the peace from her prayers caused me to face life with ease and focus. She would go into the enemy's camp and declare victory on my behalf when I had no strength to pray for myself. A mighty warrior.

What would we do without a mother? A mother teaches you how to love yourself and to be confident. She teaches you how to fight without raising your voice, but in silence, you win. Class. Intelligence. Strength. A mother teaches you how to know your place in the world and helps you realize you aren't in competition with anyone. You compete only with yourself and strive to be better each day. And when we walk in error, our mothers will remind us what truth looks like. Your mother teaches you that the benefits of getting things right are significant. Morals and values were paramount and acting out of character was not an option. Being a lady with grace and elegance was instilled in grade school. Thank God for a precious jewel, a mother.

She teaches you how to fight without raising your voice, but in silence, you win.

Think about your grandmother, how she labored in life to help you be who you are today, giving you her last and putting you first. She wanted you to be successful and second to none. Her foundation is firm, and her love is unconditional. Love and emotional openness were vital to her children's security. Her children never had to work hard and contend for love; it was just given. Love is given so freely, it makes her children model that same love to their children. Thank God for that mirror.

A mother's love is constant. She spends her time helping you through the weakest hours by pushing you forward to conquer all who oppose you. You are strong and brilliant. You don't have to wait for the world to tell you that because your mother told you first. Encouragement. Investment.

I appreciate my mother bearing my pain and facing challenges with me. She was my coach and cheerleader, reminding me I could make it no matter what it looked like or how it felt. Mothers teach you that you are stronger than the pain you are feeling, and it won't last forever. The lesson of a mother's faith and discipline has shaped many into who they are today. A mother is a protector and a nurturer. She is a gift to a child and to honor her is a joy. It is laughter; it is love, and it is favor. To honor her is life. The Word encourages children with the sweetest instruction:

> Children, obey your parents in the Lord: for this is right. Honour thy father and mother; (which is the first commandment with promise;) That it may be well with thee, and thou mayest live long on the earth (Ephesians 6:1-3).

Honoring our mothers as the Word commands blesses us with long victorious lives. We honor our mothers for the love they have demonstrated to us as children, and for the tremendous blessings they have been to our lives. Look at her hands; see how hard she has worked in life. Look into her eyes and visualize her concern for you. Listen to her talk; her wisdom will change your life. Listen to her as she shares her past mistakes, and she will teach you how to overcome. Listen to all the trials she had to conquer, and I'm sure it will encourage you to soar over the very thing you feel you can't.

The sacrifices mothers have made for their children are priceless. A devoted mother sacrifices her all for her children, and her love is endless. Should you need a friend, your mother is the best friend you could have. She will keep your secrets and give you her last so you can have more.

A schoolteacher asked a boy this question: "Suppose your mother baked a pie and there were six of you – your mother, your father, and four children. What percentage of the pie would you get?"

"One-fifth," replied the boy.

The teacher responded, "I'm afraid you don't know your fractions. Remember, there are six of you."

"I know," said the boy, "but you don't know my mother. She would say she didn't want any pie so we could have more."[1]

That's my mother. I love you, Mom.

1   https://www.preaching.com/
sermon-illustrations/illustra-
tion-mothers-sacrifice/

Words of Life

Thank You for an amazing mother who pushes me to be the best me. I'm grateful that You chose her to be my mother. I love her, Lord. I am who I am because of her love and concern for my life. I thank You, Lord, that she raised me to be a strong, God-fearing individual. Therefore, I will model that same love to my children. Lord, bless my mother for her faithfulness to me as a child. I will honor her as Your Word declares even in moments when I don't understand. I am grateful that I am here because she was here first. I thank You in faith for her long life of peace, great health, and prosperity; therefore, she will live a long satisfying life.

The Challenge

Take time out to make your mother feel special. Take her to dinner, a movie, set up a picnic, go for a walk and let her know how valuable she has been in your life.

Write down reasons why you are successful because of your mother.

PROVERB TWENTY-THREE

The
ABSOLUTE
TRUTH

I stand on it. It is my absolute truth in all matters. I can't live without it. It feeds me daily. Everything will fade away. All things will disappear, but this, I keep dear to my heart. It is so precious to me. I am made strong in weakness. Birthed from it is my confidence, character, and grace. It taught me to be strong and vigilant, lacking nothing. Each page I turn in faith comes alive in my life. I am captivated by amazing love and consumed by the faithfulness of the never changing truth. I sit in awe. It is still here. It is alive.

The Message

This Word, God's Word, is truth. His Word will last forever. When faced with trials, it is the Word of God that is the piece to life's complicated puzzle. It's the Word of God that allows us to function and not give into defeat. We are reminded of who we are through the Word, and we are not defeated because of the power of the Word. Take a minute and recall the times when you were faced with a situation, and everyone you turned to for help was lost. No one had an answer.

It was one of those dark times when you couldn't see the break of day and midnight was 24 hours long. Your situation was heavy and appeared impossible to overcome. Through the power of the Word, you could face what appeared impossible with ease and assurance knowing God was in those pages. Within the tangible pages is more than paper. Within those pages dwell life, strength, revelation, and spiritual power that equip you with the desire to live with zest and excitement. This Word is like a cannonball – you can aim and shoot it in any direction you declare. Is your loved one in trouble, sick, or incarcerated and you can't physically reach him/her? Send the Word. It flows beyond walls, through hillsides, meadows, industrial businesses, prison yards – you name it. The Word can reach your loved one.

This Word is like a cannonball – you can aim and shoot it in any direction you declare.

One of my favorite scriptures, Psalm 107:20, reads "He sent his Word and healed them, and delivered them from their destructions." When time is against you, the Word of God is faster. What would take hours and maybe even days for us, takes not even a second for God. The Word of God has power and substance. When we speak it in faith, it does not return to us void.

> So shall my word be that goeth forth out of my mouth: it shall not return unto me void, but it shall accomplish that which I please, and it shall prosper in the thing whereto I sent it (Isaiah 55:11).

Our great God is omnipotent. He owns the power to send the Word. The only word that God promises is the Word that proceeds from His mouth. God holds all authority. When you face a dire situation, speak the Word of God over it. It will not return void. It will not return empty.

While completing this chapter on April 21st, 2017 at 7:55 PM, my longtime girlfriend, Deanna, was at Stanford Hospital with her husband, Clint. While there, she texted me and a couple of ladies from our sister circle, Regina and Marika, concerned about her father who had been in surgery over 8 hours. I vividly recall her saying, "My nerves are shot. They just gave us an update, and my dad has two more hours of surgery remaining." Immediately, we all began replying with the Word of God. My text to her was, "I'm standing on the Word; it is well according to the Word of God." I really wish I could have been there with her but incredibly grateful that I could send God's Word in faith and declare her father's victorious outcome.

Because of God's omnipotence, God's people can find affirmation in the fact that the Lord's will is done on earth as it is in heaven. The outcome of that surgery was settled in heaven. Look at our God! His faithfulness never fails. At 9:44 PM, Deanna sent a text saying, "Surgery is complete, still waiting to see him. The doctor says everything went well. Amen." That Word – His Word – did not return void. Whatever we need, we can find in the Word of God. Everything. Should we need correction or to see the depth of our hearts more clearly as God sees us, the Word of God is that mirror.

> For the Word of God is quick, and powerful, and sharper than any two-edged sword, piercing even to the dividing asunder of soul and spirit, and of the joints and marrow, and is a discerner of the thoughts and intents of the heart (Hebrews 4:12).

By God's Word, we are judged. When you want to learn about yourself, spend time in His Word. When you want to know God, spend time in His Word. Read His resume. Hear His heart. Remind yourself of the promises He has for your life. The Word will make you see the error of your ways and inspire you to make changes that last. What has your thought process been like lately? What do you ruminate on throughout the night? What lives in your mind? Hebrews 4:12 challenges us to examine the things that dwell in the innermost parts of our hearts and minds. It encourages us to compare and challenge them against the Word of God for healing and deliverance.

The Word confirms we can become more like Christ, decreasing in our flesh and in our intellect. If you get lost and can't find your way, "Thy word is a lamp unto my feet, and a light unto my path" (Psalms 119:105). The lamp illuminates each step we take, and the light gives us the ability to see the areas where we should walk. I have lived enough to know undoubtedly that the Word is alive! It is our help. It is actively working in your life right now. It's more than just a book; its power enables us to be delivered from imprisonment and the bondage of the enemy who has kept many from receiving what God has for them. The Word of God will challenge you to stand and equip yourself with the confidence to tell the enemy, "Enough is enough!"

Sometimes, the devil plays on our emotions. Don't believe his falsehoods, for he takes pleasure in dishonesty. He is famous for his lies. He has an infamous past and future. The enemy will never change, but he has an expiration date. We must recognize when we are being hindered and apply the Word to our lives in faith. We realize our worth in the Word of God. The Word will carry you to the next level in your life. The Word will take you through enemy lines destroying every opponent. Bounce back! With authority, tell the devil, "I know what my situation looks like. I know what you are whispering in my ear, but God's Word declares the absolute truth in my life, and that is where my faith stands."

The enemy will never change, but he has an expiration date.

Words of Life

Father, Your Word is the center of my peace. It strengthens me in all I strive to do. I live by Your Word daily in faith. I declare Your Word as my absolute source of deliverance. I am who You say I am in Your Word. I meditate on Your Word day and night. As stated in Psalms 119:11, "Thy word have I hid in mine heart, that I might not sin against thee." Your Word makes me stand courageous and victorious. I hold fast to the principles of Your Word; therefore, I walk in power and authority. All that Your Word has said about me will not return void but will manifest in this lifetime. It is so. In Jesus' name.

The Challenge

How often do you read and study the Word of God?

What distractions do you face while reading the Word, and how could you defeat these distractions?

PROVERB TWENTY-FOUR
SILENCE

It can be so loud. So much so, it's intimidating. Silence. Nothing is heard, though it's oh, so loud causing panic, stress, and assumptions. Someone say something! Address it! Express it! No one knows how. What is this all about? If no one speaks, there is no closure to the very thing that will set one free. Break the silence.

The Message

Have you ever been here? You want to speak, but you can't find the words to express how you feel genuinely; therefore, you say nothing. Nothing makes the very thing you wanted to bring life to stay in its sunken place. No progress, no improvement, no life. You are silent because you fear if you speak, your words will be misunderstood and received in a way that is different from your intention. So, you pray. You pray that people will receive your heart and the words that flow from it. You speak in love, truth, and peace.

Have you ever asked yourself how silence nestled in between you and someone you love? Silence can cause a strain in relationships. It happens so seamlessly, so quickly, so silently. How did silence creep in and steal the very words with the power to create peace and harmony? The truth is someone stopped talking; someone gave up on trying.

God has given you a voice. Don't you dare allow the enemy to steal it! I am sure many of us have been in positions and situations where our words had the potential to set someone free. Have you been there? Did you speak?

Silence can also be a design of the enemy. Sometimes, silence is viewed as the best way to hide our flaws, faults, and insecurities. We fear rejection and become afraid to speak. Often, we struggle within ourselves and ask: "Is it even worth it? Will anyone listen? Is it worth sharing? Will it be received as authentic? Will my words be misconstrued? Is it worth vulnerability, especially to the person who caused me pain?" Allowing yourself to be vulnerable, emotionally naked, is one of the most freeing steps you can take in your quest for personal acceptance.

Silence is viewed as the best way to hide our flaws, faults, and insecurities.

I recall times in my life when I was so frustrated because I wanted to say something. I wanted to speak up and express my heart, but I didn't know how to make sense of my feelings and put them into words. I needed to speak up because I didn't want my silence to be misunderstood as acceptance. Quickly, I learned that the most important step I needed to take was to release what I held in my heart whether it was received or not. I was sure to ensure my message was expressed in love; my tone was soft and my message was shared in wisdom and truth. The experience was freeing.

I want to encourage you to speak in wisdom to set yourself free. If you let the enemy silence your voice, he takes your power and keeps you from being totally free. Reflecting on Queen Esther, she used her voice to speak on behalf of the Jewish people. She refused to remain silent; rather she used her voice to save an entire nation.

> Go gather all the Jews who are present in Shushan, and fast for me; neither eat nor drink for three days. My maids and I will fast likewise. And so I will go to the king, which is against the law; and if I perish, I perish! (Esther 4:16).

Queen Esther's voice became an instrument for restoration; she risked her life in the process. She made a persuasive request to the king to save her people. Her voice placed her in a position of royalty and favor. Esther owned her title and became an influential queen. She was destined to be royalty because of her voice and obedience. At one point in Esther's life, she listened to the voice of her uncle, Mordecai, who gave her vital instructions. Through experience and maturity, she later used her voice as a tool for the deliverance of others. Queen Esther no longer needed her uncle to speak for her. She gathered the confidence to speak up for herself knowing death would result should her words be not be accepted. She refused to be silent because of the plan of the enemy. Our voices are drowned out by the noises of the enemy; however, at a mature season in our lives, we must foster our own voices.

Don't hold back due to fear of rejection. My friends, your voice is important even though you may not see it at this time. Trust your heart and speak the very thing God has placed in your spirit. I encourage you not to be silent. Someone's deliverance depends on your voice. That broken relationship depends on your voice. Our great God needs your voice to proclaim the good news of Jesus Christ. Break the silence.

Words of Life

Father, I am thankful for the voice You have given me to speak the truth. I am no longer the same. I am free because I choose to speak and release the sentiments of my heart. I am no longer bound to silence. I thank You, Lord, for making me as bold as a lion as I rest in Your Word. I believe You created me for such a time as this to share the truth to those who walk outside of Your will. Father, I will speak Your Word with wisdom and clarity, and people's lives will be changed tremendously.

The Challenge

In prayer, write down barriers that have caused you to keep silent in the past.

Do you need help from God to break the silence about a current situation in your life? Would speaking into that situation bring deliverance to your life or others? Be honest with yourself. Ask God to help you voice your feelings with wisdom and not be silent.

PROVERB TWENTY-FIVE

GIVERS
and
TAKERS

The hand is tightly closed, and your cup remains empty. You're constantly not getting it. The reality is – you take. Give back – open that closed fist. Holding onto the little you have is not the process; the process is the power of the release.

The Message

Giving is one of the most beautiful feelings in the world. Giving from your heart looking for nothing in return is when God tremendously blesses you. Givers are those individuals who believe taking the time to give is a God-given attribute of Who God is. Jesus was sent to die for us. He gave His life that we may experience better lives. Abundant life. Sweet life of freedom. Jesus came as a ransom for you and me. He was the ultimate example of giving, a demonstration of love. We are to mirror that same love in our service to others. Have you ever stepped out in faith to bless someone, not expecting to receive anything in return? As you stepped out with a cheerful heart, you received more than you had given initially.

God loveth a cheerful giver (2 Corinthians 9:7b).

When you desire to be blessed by God, give with a cheerful heart. The blessings from heaven are accessible to you. Cheerful givers aren't predominantly giving money; they are giving blessings. Many would argue this point; it's not all about money. It truly isn't. When you sow blessings, you reap the benefits of long life, prosperity, good health, peace, joy, etc. Those who give are confident of God's future provisions for their lives. Giving is a part of praise and being obedient to God. Both produce high yields. In other words, they bear much fruit. An example was Abraham giving up his son Isaac:

> Sometime later God tested Abraham. He said to him, "Abraham!" "Here I am," he replied. Then God said, "Take your son, your only son, whom you love-Isaac-and go to the region of Moriah. Sacrifice him there as a burnt offering on a mountain I will show you." Early the next morning Abraham got up and loaded his donkey. He took with him two of his servants and his son Isaac. When he had cut enough wood for the burnt offering, he set out for the place God had told him about. On the third day Abraham looked up and saw the place in the distance. He said to his servants, "Stay here with the donkey while I and the boy go over

there. We will worship and then we will come back
to you (Genesis 22:1-5).

Abraham was tested by God but obedient. He believed and received
what God promised him. Abraham did not question the voice of God,
and God provided a ram in place of his son for the sacrifice. Abraham
trusted God, and when going up the mountain with his son, he stated,
"We will be back." He was confident in God. Are we confident? What
has God asked you to give? Did you give it? What are you willing to
sacrifice that you may, in turn, reap a bountiful harvest of blessings?
There will be a time in your life when God will test your faith. While
being tested, will you be willing to give even when you don't understand?
A powerful thought, isn't it?

What has God asked you to give? Did you give it?

Release your love, time, service, finances, and other resources so God
can bless them. When you release, watch God bless you in ways you
never imagined. Did you not know that we are trustees and stewards of
God's blessings? God desires that we share willingly to bless those who
are not as fortunate. God has blessed us magnanimously, but at times,
many tend to forget that part.

Many put God off and will say, "Tomorrow... I'll be a blessing to
others... tomorrow." You and I know that tomorrow may never come.
Our faithful God has been richly compassionate to us. God has been
faithful even when we were not faithful. He continues to shower favor
upon us. God heals, delivers, provides, and helps us to do what we

could not do for ourselves. I can't imagine life without God, can you? I wouldn't be able to make it in life without our incredible God. I would not; I would not be able to function. Life would be complicated and burdensome. Life would be confusing and chaotic. Life would be like a puzzle that has missing pieces. Lost. Empty. Strange. We owe God so much. We are to be good stewards of all that we have. Completely.

For many, their fists remain closed, and their hearts remain selfish by continually taking rather than giving. You receive favor when you give. Giving is demonstrating God's character. We live in a culture where so many take rather than give. There is no return on taking. You rob yourself of blessings when you consistently receive from God and offer Him nothing in return. Many take from others that have more than them as if they are owed that. Your mentality and perception must change.

Take a moment to reflect on all the times God has blessed you. We can't possibly number them. Now think about the times we promised God something in return. Was it time or service? Did you make a promise to the Lord? Did you keep it? God keeps His promises. Our great God has been better than good to us; nevertheless, at times we forget. The Lord has indeed kept us.

Think about the one time you were terribly sick. Think about the times you were in despair, in a dark place, and God rescued you. It was at that moment you promised God so much. You promised Him you would give Him your life. I can recall times in my life while going through some tumultuous situations that I vowed, "Lord, if You get me through this, I will serve You for the rest of my life." Does this statement sound familiar to you? It does, doesn't it? God expects us to give no matter what we are going through.

I'm sure that while going through we meant every word we promised God to the fullest. Pain and suffering will produce verbal promises without conviction. Realistically, we just want to feel better. We just want to get out of what we are experiencing. Being comfortable has a way of making us feel better and gradually, we forget what we promised. We get comfortable and complacent failing to remember that it is by God's amazing grace we remain here in the land of the living. Comfort feels good; however, it is not the time to get comfortable in the kingdom; instead, it is the time to continue being a blessing.

Pain and suffering will produce verbal promises without conviction.

As His children, we can't continue to take from God by asking Him for blessings, but sacrifice nothing ourselves. Abraham gave of his own, and he asked for nothing.

For your future progress and favor, give. And, it is never too late to come before God and expose your shortcomings. "God, I repent. I'm so sorry for the times I failed to be a blessing."

Do we sacrifice for things we love? Have you thought about how we sacrifice for things that are secondary to God? Our priorities are out of order. Let me remind you: in God we live, and move, and have our being (Acts 17:28). We need God to live, to breathe, and to remain. That is our reality. Truth. We have been living on grace so long that we make excuses for not doing what we know to be right. Excuses are just passes wrapped in lies. Grace is not a justification for excuses, but it is a conviction. Grace is a reminder of how good God is to us. We have been told for years that it is not the alarm clock that wakes us up in the morning. It is God. He gives us life, and each breath we breathe comes from Him.

Take this personally. You will know a giver versus a taker. A giver asks, "What can I do to help?" While a taker replies, "Why should I give? What's in it for me?" A giver gives unconditionally; a taker receives unconditionally. A giver expects nothing in return, while a taker expects praise and acknowledgment. We must know the difference. Be honest with yourself. Ask yourself some serious questions:

- ♥ Am I a giver or do I just take?
- ♥ Do I give praise, or do I just take compliments?
- ♥ Do I give love, or do I take a person's heart and not share my heart in return?

When you give what you have, God will take it and multiply it; you will have more than enough for yourself and others. As you release in faith, expect a river of blessings to flow your way. Trust God and be confident in your giving. God will receive your gift and bless it.

Before you place your feet on the floor in the morning say, "God, thank You that I am alive. What can I do to glorify You on the earth today?" Lord, what can I sacrifice today to be a blessing to someone in need of You?

Just as Abraham did, yield yourself to be used. Yield yourself to be a change agent for kingdom purposes.

Words of Life

Thank You, Father, for the supernatural blessings that have been bestowed upon me by being obedient to Your law of giving. I am a blessing to others, which is my heart's desire. As Your Word reminds us in Acts 20:35, "It is more blesseth to give than to receive." I give to be a blessing demonstrating who You are Lord. I am grateful for the divine favor on my life. I decree and declare that I am healed, debt free, and at peace because of what I have sown in the lives of others. Thank You, Lord, that I have received a double portion of everything I have asked of You. In Jesus' name. Amen.

The Challenge

I challenge you to give the very thing God has been asking you to give.

Be honest with yourself. What barriers caused you to be disobedient to God? Write the barriers down in order to visually see and promise yourself that these barriers won't occur again.

Declarations for a Better Tomorrow

- Don't allow situations and people to close your mouth. Don't you dare let the enemy steal your praise.

- There is a flip side to defeating the enemy. Sometimes, you must remain quiet and let God work. You don't have to respond.

- Sometimes, the very thing you are running from could be the very thing that will set you free. You will experience freedom once you face it and acknowledge that it did happen.

- Once you open your mouth and tell it, you are no longer bound by the fear of the secret.

- You are greater than your past; you are stronger than you think, but first, you must believe it.

- You are a living work on the earth, so what will you create? Someone is waiting for you to create so that they can live.

- The enemy will look at your past and study your history. However, your past is no longer who you are. No setbacks, no pitfalls.

- Unworthy and devalued by who? They are non-factors.

- Masking insecurities only make it harder for you to really get where you are going. Once you take the mask off, you can clearly see your purpose.

- Because of our sovereign God, you did not remain defeated. You soared and conquered. It's called grace.

- Grace brought you this far, so why not go even further. It only takes a made-up mind. Keep pushing with determination to win.

- Declare your freedom. Declare you are tough even when adversity stares you in the face. You have the power to keep climbing.

- Stop allowing the enemy to remind you that you failed. You didn't fail; you just needed a second chance.

- You're not drowning; you're not sinking. You just need to stay at the top and stop letting life beat you down. It's a choice, right?

- You were gracefully broken for God did not allow you to be embarrassed before others, gracefully God covered you, so your flaws would not outshine the potential before you birthed it.

- Triumphantly, you defeated your giant; no one knows what that giant is or was but you. Faith canceled out the assignment of the enemy.

- Have you ever wondered why things happen in our lives? Have you ever considered that someone else is also fighting to defeat the very thing you're fighting?

- Teach your seed to watch and pray but don't forget to teach them how to overcome and fight. It's called warfare.

- They may not know your name; however, you know your name. God knew your name before you were named.

- Your test is now a testimony; your mess is a message to others to soar, grow, prosper, smile, and to be free. To live.

- My past keeps creeping up on me Lord; I can't make it another day without You. I can breathe when I'm in Your will.

- The very thing we run from is the very thing we run back to. Don't go back to the very thing that was meant to destroy you. Just think!

- Let your voice ascend higher than the dark voices of the enemy. You have the authority so speak louder.

- Don't allow the pain of yesterday to cause you to remain stuck in negative thought patterns.

- You can't move forward by constantly rehearsing the lies the enemy has told you. Silence the voices.

- Persecution was needed to get you to the place you imagined. Now that you are here do the work.

- Old wounds can be brilliant stories when we decide to speak from a place of healing, rather than a place of pity.

- That relationship wasn't good for you; however, it made you better. Better than you were yesterday.

- Don't let the other kind of pride cause you to lose when you are winning. Stay humble.

- Take those shackles off and live better than yesterday!

- Refuse to be a hostage to other's opinions. Change the channel in your mind because people will capitalize on your pain and turn it into punishment.

Conclusion

Because the enemy constantly reminds us of past mistakes, pain, fears, and insecurities, we must remind the enemy that our God is greater than his strategies. The enemy works hard to keep us ineffective and bound by thoughts, emotions, and past experiences. It is my prayer that this book of proverbs does damage to the kingdom of the enemy. I've challenged you to read this compilation of proverbs from my heart to yours, and let it change your life significantly. When you receive the wisdom God has for you, you are a threat to the enemy's kingdom and an effective witness for God's glory. Our great God desires us to be free and live in victory! The designs of the enemy will not detour you from your promising future. Don't let the enemy of your past keep you stuck in your yesterday. It's time to live! Doing so is a choice only you can make. I leave you with this poem by Heartsill Wilson:

> This is the beginning of a new day. God has given me this day to use as I will. I can waste it or use it for good. What I do today is very important because I am exchanging a day of my life for it. When tomorrow comes, this day will be gone forever, leaving something in its place I have traded for it. I want it to be gain, not loss – good, not evil. Success, not failure in order that I shall not forget the price I paid for it.[1]

---

1 https://www.truthorfiction.com/alabama-coach-paul-bear-bryant-carried-a-prayer-in-his-wallet/

Special Thanks

Your guidance, creativity, patience, professionalism, and expertise exceeded my expectations. Christian Living Books, I am in awe of the work produced. You made my dream come to life. I'm exceedingly grateful.

God couldn't have given me a better person to assist me. Sheila Joseph, you were faithful in helping me to succeed with this assignment from God. Your constant dedication and unselfish sacrifice meant so much to me. Your spirit of excellence blessed this book. When I became anxious, you constantly reminded me that it was all in God's timing and excellence was the key. I thank you!

You saw the gift of writing in me from the beginning. Mrs. Sheryl Brown, your perception, and direction with this assignment from God blossomed to greatness. I appreciate your prayers.

Your intelligence is a gift. Alexis Kemp, my baby girl. You are simply the best. While carrying 18 units in college and serving as a basketball manager, you helped mom to complete the editing. Alexandria Kemp, thank you for a creative mindset; You gave me the title for Proverb Nineteen and helped me to see the millennial's perspective. I thank you, daughters.

For your willingness to help, lovingly, I'm grateful, Nakeisha Moya, Crystal Butler McQueen, and Sabrina Roberts. Thank you for sacrificing your time reading and reviewing when I needed you.

Your support and originality produced beautifully. It's a great feeling when your brother takes excellent photographs, and your picture lands on the cover of your first book. Mr. Daniel and Mrs. Geneva Jordan of D Jordan Photographic, I thank you for believing in me.

Special Acknowledgements

To my entire, beloved family, and my dear brothers, I love you so much. The gift of family is priceless. I honor you.

To Joy Perkins and Greater Harvest Christian Women of Faith and Fellowship, you are my heart. To my Harvest Church Family, thank you for the prayers and amazing support. I feel blessed to be the vessel that God chose to lead you. I love you dearly.

To my son, Javon Kemp, your excitement for this assignment from God melts my heart and I am so glad we are better than yesterday. Thank you for always listening. Your love for me as a mom warms my heart. I love you.

To my sisterhood, Deanna, Marika, Regina, Tonya, Stacey, Shawn, and Michelle, of 35 plus years of friendship, our village is strong from elementary school to adulthood. We are forever connected. We will grow older, stronger and wiser together. Proverb Ten is dedicated to you.

To Raquel Elish Browden, I am no longer a dandelion but a powerful rose. Thank you for that simple text message of your thoughts of me. Who would have ever thought that text would create the framework for the introduction to my first book. I am forever your Naomi.

To Brandon Shelton, for your faithfulness in challenging me with thoughts. Your timing was always right on time. I appreciate you.

To First Lady Kimberly Watkin and Minister Marisa Banks, I'm thankful for our garden. There's so much planted there, and up came a rose. Thank you for your truth and commitment to me during this entire assignment from God and years later, we are finally here.

To Genetra Richardson, for all the late nights you listened to me read for hours, and you never complained. Thank you for staying awake. I appreciate the excitement while I read to you.

To Chloe Wesson and Nathalie Seward, we have spent so many months talking about this book while working together. You, too, have always listened and encouraged me to finish. We made it through some rough days, talking about the Lord together. I appreciate you so much.

To La'Drea Luckey, my talented niece, your gift of writing and perception inspired me to write. I thank you for listening and encouraging me on this journey.

To Gilbert Graim, my heart. Your steadfast love towards me is real. There's nothing you wouldn't do for me.

To Cynthia Boyd, we have shared so much together through the years. There's so much you have helped me in ministry to accomplish. You answer every phone call and email. You are a faithful, kind and loving assistant. Everything I put my hands on you helped me to perfect. I thank you.

To my nail technician, Talia Hill. Your clients love visiting and sharing with their favorite nail lady. Talia, I could never get out of your shop because were both crying, laughing, preaching and loving on each other. We have talked about *Better than Yesterday* forever. Finally, it is here! Thank you for your sweet fellowship. By faith, you are better than yesterday.

To my First Lady Sisters and dearest friends, I love you so much. I'm blessed to have you in my life. To those who have prayed for me through the years and offered love, I thank you. I can't simply name all of you. I am most grateful for those who have helped me along this writing journey; you know who you are. Thank you for encouraging me to write. With much love and God, I did it. I humbled and thankful.

This book would not be possible without the one above. Thank you, Jesus, for being the best thing that ever happened to my life. I thank you, Lord, for loving me and transforming my life into wholeness. I am a testament to your favor and grace. I give You all the glory.

About the Author

LADY VICKI LYNNE KEMP was born to the late Pastor Daniel and Evangelist Cora Jordan. She was the last of five children to this union and the only girl. She has been married to her friend, Pastor Vernon Kemp, for 26 years. Lady Kemp has gracefully and humbly served with her husband at Greater Harvest Christian Center, Church of God in Christ for seventeen years. God has blessed this union with gifted and anointed children.

Lady Kemp exemplifies the love of God and undoubtedly embodies the Proverbs 31 woman. Her favorite scripture is Psalm 91:1:

> He that dwelleth in the secret place of the most High shall abide under the shadow of the Almighty.

This scripture resonates with her spirit and the calling on her life. She encourages the people of God to embrace the "secret place" and experience the power of prayer. Through God's healing power, she testifies that "prayer works." Lady Kemp serves as the Women's Ministry Administrator; she has a passion for encouraging women to be stronger emotionally, mentally and spiritually. She also provides leadership on the Board of Scholastic Education of Greater Harvest Christian Center where she devotes her time developing educational strategies to help students WIN. She serves on the Board of Directors of Bakersfield Senior Center of Kern County.

For the past 16 years, she has been a full-time employee for Kern Regional Center in Bakersfield, CA where she is a Service Coordinator for the Special Needs population of Kern County. Lady Kemp earned a Bachelor of Arts degree in Liberal Studies in 1996 from California State University, Bakersfield.

Lady Kemp received her Evangelist license in December of 2004. God has graced her to travel and minister the Gospel of Jesus Christ. Along with her spiritual accomplishments, God has given Lady Kemp a vision to serve and foster youth within the community in the area of education as the founder of Harvest of Hope Educational Services which was birthed on August 9, 2016. This educational component is a branch of Greater Harvest Christian Center. Lady Kemp loves young people and yields herself to be a vessel used by God for His glory. She has a Kingdom Agenda to reach lost souls for Christ while also challenging and empowering youth to be successful in education. Her unwavering faith, compassion, selflessness, and incessant prayers speak volumes of her character and epitomize an undeniable and genuine love for God and for His people. Lady Kemp's favorite statement is, "There is absolutely nothing too hard for our great God." If you believe you can, by faith, you will.

Connect with Lady Kemp

Twitter – @LadyVKemp

IG – LadyVickiLKemp

Facebook – Vicki Kemp

Website – vickilynnekemp.com

Business Email – Kempvicki@aol.com

Sign up for my weekly motivational email list at uarebetterthanyesterday@gmail.com.

CPSIA information can be obtained
at www.ICGtesting.com
Printed in the USA
LVHW011502160623
749998LV00007B/857

9 781562 293604